# Easy WordPerfect® for Windows™

## for Version 5.2

Shelley O'Hara

# Easy WordPerfect for Windows for Version 5.2

**Easy WordPerfect for Windows for Version 5.2**
**Copyright © 1993 by Que® Corporation**

All rights reserved. Printed in the United States of America. No part of this book may be used or reproduced in any form or by any means, or stored in a database or retrieval system, without prior written permission of the publisher except in the case of brief quotations embodied in critical articles and reviews. Making copies of any part of this book for any purpose other than your own personal use is a violation of United States copyright laws. For information, address Que Corporation, 11711 N. College Ave., Carmel, IN 46032.

Library of Congress Catalog No.: 92-82061

ISBN 1-56529-126-3

This book is sold *as is*, without warranty of any kind, either express or implied, respecting the contents of this book, including but not limited to implied warranties for the book's quality, performance, merchantability, or fitness for any particular purpose. Neither Que Corporation nor its dealers or distributors shall be liable to the purchaser or any other person or entity with respect to any liability, loss, or damage caused or alleged to have been caused directly or indirectly by this book.

95  94        6  5  4  3  2

Interpretation of the printing code: the rightmost double-digit number is the year of the book's printing; the rightmost single-digit number, the number of the book's printing. For example, a printing code of 93-1 shows that the first printing of the book occurred in 1993.

Screen reproductions in this book were created using Collage Plus from Inner Media, Inc., Hollis, NH.

*Easy WordPerfect for Windows for Version 5.2* is based on WordPerfect 5.2 for Windows.

*Publisher:* Lloyd J. Short

*Operations Manager:* Sheila Cunningham

*Book Design:* Scott Cook

*Production Team*: Debra Adams, Claudia Bell, Phil Kitchel, Bob LaRoche, Jay Lesandrini, Caroline Roop, Johnna Van Hoose, Kelli Widdifield

The text in this book is printed on recycled paper.

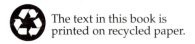

# Credits

**Production Editor**
Cindy Morrow

**Technical Editor**
Jerry Ellis

**Novice Reviewer**
Stacey Beheler

---

Microsoft Windows is a registered trademark of Microsoft Corporation.

WordPerfect is a registered trademark of WordPerfect Corporation.

# About the Author

Shelley O'Hara is a Title Manager at Que Corporation. She is the author of 17 books in the *Easy* series, including the best-selling *Easy WordPerfect*, *Easy Windows*, and *Easy 1-2-3*. She is also the co-author of *Real Men Use DOS*. Ms. O'Hara received her Bachelors Degree from the University of South Carolina and her Masters Degree from the University of Maryland.

# Contents

**Introduction** ............................................................. 1

    What Is WordPerfect for Windows? ................................ 2

    How This Book Is Organized ........................................ 2

    How To Use This Book ................................................ 4

    How To Follow an Exercise ........................................... 4

**The Basics** .................................................................. 9

    Using a Mouse ......................................................... 10

    Understanding Your Keyboard ..................................... 11

        The Function Keys .............................................. 11

        Other Special Keys ............................................. 12

    Understanding the Document Screen ........................... 13

    Selecting a Menu Command ....................................... 14

    Moving the Insertion Point ......................................... 17

    Typing Text ............................................................. 18

    Understanding Reveal Codes ...................................... 18

    Saving and Retrieving Your Work ................................. 19

**Task/Review** ............................................................. 21

    Alphabetical Listing of Tasks ....................................... 22

    Entering and Editing Text ........................................... 25

        Start WordPerfect for Windows ............................. 26

        Select a menu command ..................................... 28

        Exit WordPerfect for Windows .............................. 30

        Get help ........................................................... 32

        Add text ........................................................... 34

v

# Contents

 Overwrite text ........................................................... 36

 Insert a blank line .................................................... 38

 Combine paragraphs .............................................. 40

 Insert a tab .............................................................. 42

 Enter a page break ................................................. 44

 Go to a page ........................................................... 46

 Select text ............................................................... 48

 Delete text ............................................................... 50

 Undelete text .......................................................... 52

 Copy text ................................................................. 54

 Move text ................................................................ 56

 Use Undo ................................................................ 58

**Working with Files** ........................................................ 61

 Save a document for the first time ....................... 62

 Save a document again ......................................... 64

 Save a document with a new name ..................... 66

 Save and close a document .................................. 68

 Abandon changes .................................................. 70

 Open a document ................................................... 72

 Display files in a different directory ..................... 74

 Create a new document ........................................ 76

 Save selected text .................................................. 78

 Combine two documents ...................................... 80

 Open more than one document ........................... 82

 Display more than one document ........................ 84

# Contents

    Make a different document active ........................86

    Delete a file.................................................................88

**Basic Formatting** ..............................................................91

    Display Reveal Codes................................................92

    Center text..................................................................94

    Indent text..................................................................96

    Create a hanging indent..........................................98

    Align text flush right ..............................................100

    Boldface text............................................................102

    Underline text..........................................................104

    Italicize text .............................................................106

    Change the font......................................................108

    Change the font size..............................................110

**Advanced Editing and Formatting** .............................113

    Insert the date .........................................................114

    Search for text ........................................................116

    Search and replace text .........................................118

    Check spelling ........................................................122

    Use the thesaurus ..................................................124

    Count words............................................................126

    Alphabetize text......................................................128

    Change the case of text ........................................130

    Display the Ruler ...................................................132

    Display the Button Bar ..........................................134

    Set tabs ....................................................................136

# Contents

    Double-space a document ................................. 138

    Set margins ....................................................... 140

    Number pages .................................................. 142

    Create a header ................................................ 144

    Edit a header .................................................... 146

    Create a footer ................................................. 148

    Edit a footer ..................................................... 150

    Center a page ................................................... 152

    Draw a horizontal line ...................................... 154

    Insert a special character .................................. 156

    Insert a graphic ................................................ 158

    Move a graphic ................................................. 160

    Insert a table .................................................... 162

    Enter text into a table ...................................... 164

**Printing** ............................................................... 167

    Select a printer ................................................ 168

    Preview a document ......................................... 170

    Display a document in Draft mode .................... 172

    Print the on-screen document ........................... 174

    Print selected text ............................................ 176

**Merging** .............................................................. 179

    Create a merge letter ....................................... 180

    Create a secondary file ..................................... 182

    Enter a record into the secondary file ................ 186

    Enter other records into the secondary file ....... 188

Save the secondary file ........................................ 190

Create a primary file ............................................. 192

Save the primary file ............................................. 196

Merge the files ...................................................... 198

**Reference** ................................................................ **201**

Formatting Codes ................................................... 202

Keyboard Guide ...................................................... 203

    To open a menu ................................................. 203

    To select a menu command ............................. 203

    To select an option in a dialog box ................. 203

    To select text .................................................... 203

Glossary ................................................................... 204

Where To Get More Help ...................................... 208

**Index** ............................................................................ **209**

# Introduction

*Easy* **WordPerfect for Windows**

# Introduction

## What Is WordPerfect for Windows?

WordPerfect for Windows is the Microsoft Windows version of one of the world's most popular word processing software programs. You can use the program to create a variety of documents:

- Letters
- Memos
- Reports
- Manuscripts
- Term papers
- Legal documents
- Proposals
- Outlines
- Press releases
- Resumes
- Form letters

## How This Book Is Organized

All of WordPerfect's features make working with text easy. Using this program saves you time and makes your work more efficient. But learning to use the many features is difficult at first. That's why you need this book.

This book is designed to make learning WordPerfect *easy*. This book helps the beginning WordPerfect user perform basic operations. Following the step-by-step instructions, you can learn how to take advantage of the editing and formatting options of WordPerfect.

2/13/93

Eric VanDyke
5301 North Main Street
Indianapolis, IN 46205

Dear Mr. VanDyke:

Thank you for agreeing to be present at the dedica...
building. As one of the most outstanding athletes t...
represent our commitment to athletic excellence.

We look forward to seeing you on April 4.

Thank you,


Michael R. Burns
Athletic Director

---

**GET OUT YOUR CHECKERED FLAG!**

**IT'S THAT TIME AGAIN!**

**JOIN US FOR THE 7TH ANNUAL RACE DAY PARTY!**

DATE:   RACE DAY

TIME:   AFTER THE RACE

PLACE:  5509 SOUTH TEMPLE

...ROVIDED. PLEASE BRING A
...BAKED BEANS, COLE SLAW,
...OR SOMETHING).

---

### Ramen Noodles and Lawrence Welk

I still haven't learned the fine art of grocery shopping. My friends at work are always bewildered at why I refuse to cook. "Oh, it's *ea-sy*," my friend Martha tells me. "You can throw a steak in a frying pan, sprinkle some seasoned salt on it, steam a couple of vegetables, and you've got a great meal." True, but you first have to think to buy the steak and the vegetables and then take the time to cook and steam them. That's the problem: I go for the instant gratification—toaster pastries, chicken noodle soup, instant mashed potato mix. Tonight the store had a seven-for-a-dollar sale on Ramen noodles. I bought three dollars' worth.

I instantly opened a package of the pork-flavored kind when I got home. The pungent bouillon smell made me happy...
and in the middle of my last year of coll...
rented that awful one-bedroom flat. As ...
water, I could see the patriotic "Spirit of...
the cracked kitchen linoleum beneath m...
and was wearing dangling earrings and ...

Amy Jo Evans first introduced me to Ra...
ways to make our individual seven-doll...
all the necessities, like Swiss Chip Lite i...
one day saying she'd heard about a "ne...

Ramen noodles became a staple in our ...
at four and fix herself and package that ...
talk show. Then I'd come home at arou...
chicken, the pork smell from hers still li...

Amy Jo DeHart introduced me to Lawr...
year I was hauling crates of paint aroun...
custom-mixing colors for patrons and t...
Chaucer textbook and a couple of dome...
her summer writing for a local paper an...
our abode. By the time the school year ...
of treasures that we piled in our living r...
holder, 15-year-old family portraits, a v...
ball inscribed with the name "Clara."

Mid-summer, however, the thrust of he...
Saturday nights, as she was perched be...
reruns with her parents. I spent my enti...
should bring a vacuum cleaner. She wo...
theme on Lawrence Welk.

I learned that the Lawrence Welk show ...

---

### Division Summary

Shop America's two divisions, Rebels and BullDog Wear, both showed an increase in catalog and retail sales. New stores were opened for each retail chain, which helped increase retail sales. The catalogs were redesigned, which contributed to an increase in catalog sales.

Rebels is an exclusive clothing store for men and women. The chain strives to include designs and clothing that customers cannot find elsewhere. BullDog Wear is an established force in the casual wear market. This chain supplies all-cotton clothing for all ages.

### Sales

Both catalog sales and retail store sales increased this year. Here's a breakdown of sales (in millions):

|               | 1991 | 1992 |
|---------------|------|------|
| Catalog Sales | 2.2  | 2.8  |
| Retail Stores | 1.4  | 1.8  |
| Total         | 3.6  | 4.6  |

### New Stores

In 1992, eleven new retail stores were added. Here's a breakdown of the location of the new stores:

| Store | Location |
|-------|----------|
| Rebels | Washington, D.C |
|  | Charleston, SC |
|  | Philadelphia, PA |
|  | Tampa, FL |
|  | Cincinnati, OH |
| BullDog Wear | Indianapolis, IN |
|  | Holland, MI |
|  | Chicago, IL |

Annual Report, January 5, 1993                    Page 1

---

**Introduction**

This book is designed with you, the beginner, in mind. The book is divided into several parts:

| Part | Function |
| --- | --- |
| Introduction | Explains how the book is set up and how to use the book. |
| The Basics | Explains basic concepts you need to know to get started. |
| Task/Review | Explains how to perform particular tasks. |
| Reference | Includes a keyboard guide and a glossary. |

## How To Use This Book

This book is set up so that you can use it several different ways:

- You can read the book from start to finish. Or you can pick up the book and begin reading at any point in the text.
- You can look up specific tasks that you want to accomplish, such as making text bold, in the alphabetical list of tasks.
- You can flip through the book, looking at the Before and After screens, to find specific tasks.
- You can read just the exercise, just the review, or both the exercise and review sections.
- You can read any part of the exercises. You can read all the text to see both the steps to follow and the explanation of the steps. You can read just the text in red to see the commands to select and keystrokes to press. You can read just the explanation to understand what happens during a particular step.

## How To Follow an Exercise

WordPerfect is flexible because it enables you to perform a task many different ways. For consistency, this book makes certain assumptions about how your computer is set up and how you use WordPerfect. As you follow along with each exercise, keep the following key points in mind:

- This book assumes that you have a hard drive and that you followed the basic installation. This book assumes that you have installed a printer and that you have not changed any program defaults.

- This book assumes that you use the mouse to select text, to move the insertion point, to select menu commands, and so on. Remember that you also can use the keyboard to accomplish these tasks. (For more information, see the "Keyboard Guide" in the Reference part.)

- In the exercise sections, this book assumes that you are starting from the Before screen. If this screen contains any text, you should type the text as it appears.

- Only the Before and After screens are illustrated. The book does not shows screens for every step within an exercise. Where necessary, the steps discuss screen messages and how to respond to them.

- So that you can read all the text on the screens, this book uses a large on-screen typeface. Depending on the typeface you select, your screen and line breaks might look different than they appear in this book.

## Task section

The Task section includes numbered steps that tell you how to accomplish certain tasks, such as combining two documents. The numbered steps walk you through a specific example so that you can learn the task by doing it. Blue text below the numbered steps explains the concept in more detail.

## Oops! notes

You might find that you performed a task that you do not want after all. The Oops! notes tell you how to undo each procedure or how to get out of a situation. By showing you how to reverse nearly every procedure, these notes enable you to use WordPerfect more confidently.

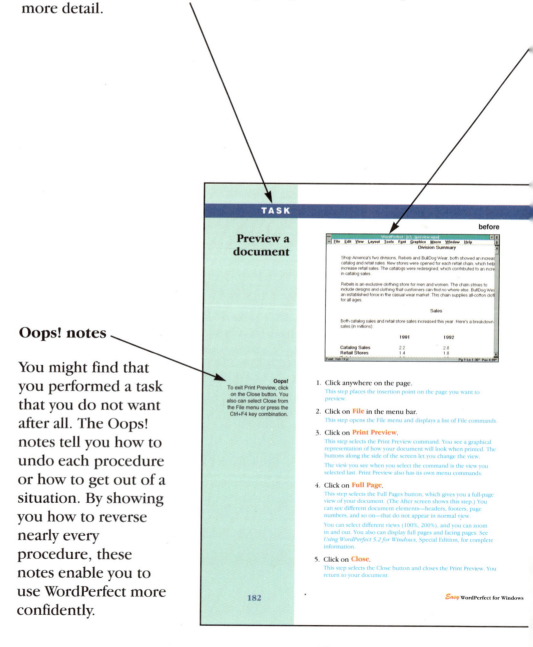

## Before and After screens

Each task includes Before and After screens that show how the computer screen will look before and after you follow the numbered steps in the Task section.

## Other notes

The extra margin notes explain a little more about each procedure. These notes define terms, explain other options, and refer you to other sections, when applicable.

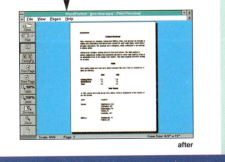

after

**Try a shortcut**
Press the Shift+F5 key combination to select the Print Preview command.

## Review section

After you learn a procedure by following a specific example, you can refer to the Review section for a quick summary of the task. The Review section gives you the generic steps for completing a task so that you can apply them to your own work. You can use these steps as a quick reference to refresh your memory about how to perform procedures.

### REVIEW

1. Click on **File** in the menu bar.
2. Click on the **Print Preview** command.
3. If you want to change the view, click on **View** in the menu bar; then click on the view you want. Or click on **Pages**, and select a page option.
4. Click on the **Close** button to exit Print Preview.

**To preview a document**

*See other pages*
To view other pages, select the Next Page or Prev Page buttons.

Printing

183

Introduction

7

# The Basics

Using a Mouse

Understanding Your Keyboard

Understanding the Document Screen

Selecting a Menu Command

Moving the Insertion Point

Typing Text

Understanding Reveal Codes

Saving and Retrieving Your Work

*Easy* **WordPerfect for Windows**

# The Basics

**Using the keyboard**
Using the keyboard is covered in the "Keyboard Guide" in the Reference part.

## Using a Mouse

Using the mouse is the easiest and most natural way to learn WordPerfect and other Microsoft Windows programs. This book assumes that you are using a mouse.

When you move the mouse on the desk, the mouse pointer moves on-screen. You can use the mouse to

- Select menu commands (see "Selecting a Menu Command")
- Select text

There are several types of mouse actions, including the following:

| Term | Action |
| --- | --- |
| Point | Position the mouse pointer on an item. Be sure that the tip of the arrow is on the item. |
| Click | Point to an item, press the left mouse button, and then release the mouse button. |
| Double-click | Point to an item and press the left mouse button twice in rapid succession. |
| Drag | Point to an item. Press and hold down the left mouse button, and then move the mouse. After the item you are dragging is positioned where you want it, release the mouse button. |

**Nothing happens?**
If you double-click the mouse and nothing happens, you might not have clicked quickly enough and the computer interpreted the double-click as two single clicks. Try again.

10

*Easy* WordPerfect for Windows

Keep these terms in mind as you follow the tasks in this book.

## Understanding Your Keyboard

A computer keyboard is just like a typewriter, only a keyboard has additional keys:

- Function keys (F1 through F10 or F1 through F12, depending on your keyboard)
- Other special keys, such as Esc, Del, Ins

These keys are located in different places on different keyboards. For example, sometimes the function keys are located across the top of the keyboard. Sometimes they are located on the left side of the keyboard.

### The Function Keys

If you want, you can use the function keys rather than the mouse to select commands. Pressing the F3 key, for example, selects the File Save As command. For some commands, you use a key combination—the function key and a modifier key.

Shift is an example of a modifier key. You're probably familiar with the Shift key from a typewriter. You press Shift and t, for instance, to create a different letter—uppercase T.

You use the Shift key in the same way with the function key—you press it to access a different command than the function key alone would access.

Alt and Ctrl are special modifier keys. They work just like Shift. Pressing Alt and a function key, for example, accesses a different command than pressing the function key alone would access.

To press any key, tap the key once. (Some keys will repeat if you hold them down too long.) To use a key combination, press and hold down the first key; then press the second key. Key combinations in this book are indicated with a plus sign (+). If the steps tell you to press Alt+F3, for example, you would press and hold the Alt key, press the F3 key, and then release both keys.

The WordPerfect menu lists keyboard shortcuts. Also, this book covers some shortcuts in the exercises of the Task/Review part. For more information about keyboard shortcuts, see the Quick Reference guide on the inside front cover of this book.

## Other Special Keys

Your keyboard also contains other special keys. Here's a short list of these keys:

| Key | Function |
| --- | --- |
| Backspace | Deletes the character to the left of the insertion point. |
| Ins | Toggles between Typeover and Insert mode. |
| Del | Deletes the character to the right of the insertion point. |
| Esc | Enables you to back out of situations—close a menu without making a selection, close a dialog box, and so on. |
| Shift | When used with arrow keys, enables you to select text. |

## Understanding the Document Screen

After you start the program, you see a blank document window. (If you want to start the program and follow along, see *TASK: Start WordPerfect for Windows*, which is the first task in the Task/Review part.)

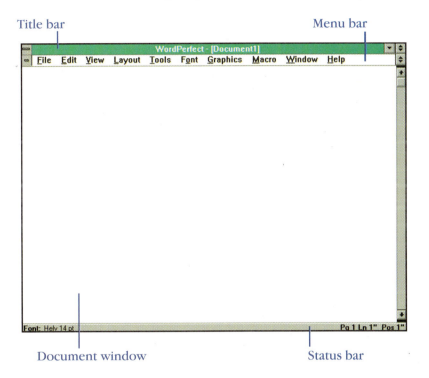

You might be intimidated at first when you see this blank screen. Just think of the screen as a blank piece of paper. You can write anything you want—just start typing.

The *title bar*, which is the first line on-screen, displays the name of the document. If you haven't saved (and named) the document, the word Document1 appears in the title bar.

The *menu bar* is under the title bar. This line displays the main menu names (File, Edit, View, Layout, Tools, Font, Graphics, Macro, Window, and Help). To select a menu command, see "Selecting a Menu Command."

The *document window* appears under the menu bar. It is the area where you type text.

**See Ruler and Button Bar?**
Your screen also might contain a Ruler and Button Bar. You can choose whether to display or hide the Ruler and Button Bar (see *TASK: Display the Button Bar* and *TASK: Display the Ruler*).

**Can't move insertion point?**
Notice that when the screen is blank, you cannot use the mouse or the arrow keys to move the insertion point. WordPerfect does not let you move the insertion point where nothing exists. After you type text, however, you can move the insertion point.

The *status bar* is the last line on-screen. This line displays information about the current mode and about the location of the insertion point. The lower right side of the status bar displays this information about your document:

| Indicator | Description |
|---|---|
| Pg | Page number |
| Ln | Line number in inches (the insertion point's vertical position, measured from the top of the page) |
| Pos | Cursor position in inches (the insertion point's horizontal position, measured from the left edge of the page) |

## Selecting a Menu Command

You access commands through the menu system of WordPerfect. Click on the menu that you want to open—for instance, File. You see a list of commands. Click on the command that you want.

**Close a menu**
You may display a menu that you don't want. To leave a menu without making a selection, press the Esc key.

When you select a command that has an arrow following the command name, an additional menu appears. This additional menu—called a *cascading menu*—lists other commands or options. To select a command from a cascading menu, click on the command.

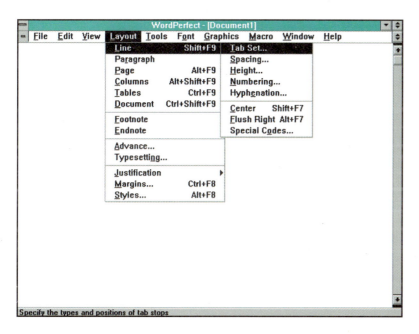

When a command is followed by ellipsis (...), you must specify additional options before you initiate the command. When you select the command, a dialog box appears. The dialog box might ask you to enter text, make a choice about options, or confirm an operation. When you select the File Open command, for example, the Open File dialog box appears.

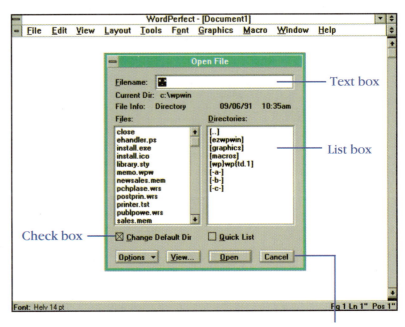

Dialog boxes can contain different elements. Each item might require a different type of selection process. Here are some of the most common elements:

*Text box.* A box within a dialog box. You type information (such as the file name) into this box. To select a text box, click in the box. (Sometimes the insertion point is already positioned in the text box.)

*Check box.* A square box that appears in a dialog box. Check boxes can be checked (selected) or unchecked (unselected). To select a check box, click in the box. To unselect a check box, click in that box again. A check box is selected if an X appears in it.

*List box.* A list of available choices—such as file names or directories. To select an item in a list, click on it. Sometimes list boxes have scroll bars that you can use to scroll through the list by clicking on the up or down scroll arrow.

*Option button.* A round button that appears in a dialog box. To select an option, click in the option button. A dot appears in the button. You cannot activate more than one option button at a time in a dialog box. (An option button is not shown in the figure.)

*Command button.* A choice of action that appears in a dialog box. Two common command buttons are OK and Cancel. To select a command button, click on it. Most dialog boxes have a "default" command or option button, which has a thicker border than the other buttons. To select this button, you can also press Enter.

## Moving the Insertion Point

To move the insertion point by using the mouse, move the mouse pointer on-screen to where you want to place the insertion point. Then click the mouse button.

Notice that if there is nothing on-screen, you cannot move the insertion point. WordPerfect doesn't let you move the insertion point where nothing exists. After you have entered text (or graphics) on-screen, you can move the insertion point.

You can use the arrow keys and other key combinations to move the insertion point. Here is a list of the most common keys:

| To move | Press |
| --- | --- |
| One character right | → |
| One character left | ← |
| One line up | ↑ |
| One line down | ↓ |
| Previous word | Ctrl+← |
| Next word | Ctrl+→ |

*continues*

**Use the keyboard**
You can also use the keyboard to select menu commands. See the "Keyboard Guide" in the Reference part.

| To move | Press |
|---|---|
| Beginning of line | Home |
| End of line | End |
| Beginning of document | Ctrl+Home |
| End of document | Ctrl+End |
| Top of screen | PgUp |
| Bottom of screen | PgDn |

## Typing Text

To enter text, just start typing. The alphanumeric keys work just as they do on a typewriter. Instead of committing the characters to paper, however, you see what you type on-screen. Note that unlike a typewriter, you do not have to press Enter when you reach the end of a line. If WordPerfect cannot fit a word on a line, it ends the line and moves the word to the next line. This feature is referred to as *word wrap*.

## Understanding Reveal Codes

Many times when you select a command, WordPerfect inserts a hidden code into your text. These codes can indicate tab stops, margin settings, hard returns, typeface changes, and so on. When you use these features, you don't have to worry about the codes. WordPerfect inserts them automatically.

If you need to change the effects of these features, you need to be able to display and delete the codes.

To display hidden codes, select Reveal Codes from the View menu (or press the Alt+F3 key combination). The screen splits in half with the same text displayed in both windows. The lower part of the screen shows the hidden codes. The insertion point also appears in both screens. When you move the insertion point, it moves in sync in both screens.

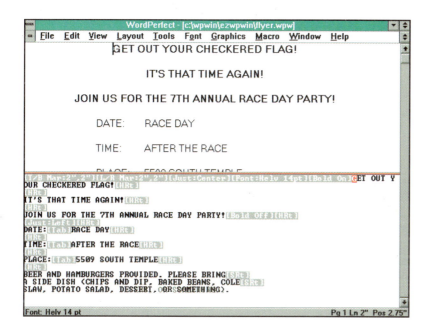

To delete a code, open the Reveal Codes window, use the mouse or the arrow keys to move the insertion point to the code, and then press the Del key.

Generally, you can guess what a code does by what appears in the Reveal Codes window. For instance, `[Ln Spacing: 2]` tells you that a code to change line spacing has been inserted. Don't worry about memorizing all the codes. The important and common codes will become familiar to you as you use them. The Quick Reference on the inside front cover lists some of the most common codes.

To restore the document window to full-size, select Reveal Codes from the View menu (or press the Alt+F3 key combination).

See *TASK: Display Reveal Codes* for more information.

## Saving and Retrieving Your Work

All your work is stored temporarily in memory, which is like having a shopping list in your head. Until you commit the list to paper, you might forget some or all of the items. The same is true with WordPerfect. Until you save the document, you can lose all or part of your work.

Saving the document doesn't commit it to paper like the shopping list. Saving the document saves the document to a disk. Then when you need the document again, you can retrieve it from the disk.

WordPerfect does not save your work automatically. You should save every 5 or 10 minutes. If you don't save your work, you could lose it. Suppose that you have been working on a document for a few hours. Then your power is turned off unexpectedly—an air conditioning repair person at your office shorts out the power, or a thunderstorm hits. Any number of calamities can cause a power loss. If you haven't saved your document, you will lose all your hard work.

**Use backup feature**
You can turn on a backup feature that saves your work for you. See *Using WordPerfect 5.2 for Windows*, Special Edition, for information.

You have many choices when you save a document. Refer to these tasks:

| *When you want to* | *Refer to* |
| --- | --- |
| Save a document that you have not saved | TASK: *Save a document for the first time* |
| Open a document that you have saved | TASK: *Open a document* |
| Save a document that you have already saved | TASK: *Save a document again* |
| Save a document with a new name; keep the original document | TASK: *Save a document with a new name* |
| Start a new document | TASK: *Create a new document* |
| Clear the screen and abandon the document on-screen; return to the previous version (if you have saved) or lose the current version (if you haven't saved) | TASK: *Abandon changes* |
| Clear the screen, but save the document | TASK: *Save and close a document* |

# Task/Review

Entering and Editing Text

Working with Files

Basic Formatting

Advanced Editing and Formatting

Printing

Merging

*Easy* **WordPerfect for Windows**

# Alphabetical Listing of Tasks

Abandon changes ............................................................. 70
Add text ............................................................................ 34
Align text flush right ..................................................... 100
Alphabetize text ............................................................. 128
Boldface text .................................................................. 102
Center a page ................................................................. 152
Center text ....................................................................... 94
Change the case of text ................................................. 130
Change the font ............................................................. 108
Change the font size ..................................................... 110
Check spelling ............................................................... 122
Combine paragraphs ...................................................... 40
Combine two documents ............................................... 80
Copy text .......................................................................... 54
Count words .................................................................. 126
Create a footer ............................................................... 148
Create a hanging indent ................................................. 98
Create a header ............................................................. 144
Create a merge letter .................................................... 180
Create a new document .................................................. 76
Create a primary file .................................................... 192
Create a secondary file ................................................. 182
Delete a file ..................................................................... 88
Delete text ........................................................................ 50
Display a document in Draft mode .............................. 172
Display files in a different directory ............................. 74
Display more than one document ................................. 84
Display Reveal Codes ..................................................... 92
Display the Button Bar ................................................. 134
Display the Ruler .......................................................... 132
Double-space a document ........................................... 138
Draw a horizontal line ................................................. 154
Edit a footer .................................................................. 150
Edit a header ................................................................. 146
Enter a page break .......................................................... 44
Enter a record into the secondary file ........................ 186
Enter other records into the secondary file ............... 188
Enter text into a table ................................................... 164
Exit WordPerfect for Windows ...................................... 30

22

| | |
|---|---|
| Get help | 32 |
| Go to a page | 46 |
| Indent text | 96 |
| Insert a blank line | 38 |
| Insert a graphic | 158 |
| Insert a special character | 156 |
| Insert a tab | 42 |
| Insert a table | 162 |
| Insert the date | 114 |
| Italicize text | 106 |
| Make a different document active | 86 |
| Merge the files | 198 |
| Move a graphic | 160 |
| Move text | 56 |
| Number pages | 142 |
| Open a document | 72 |
| Open more than one document | 82 |
| Overwrite text | 36 |
| Preview a document | 170 |
| Print selected text | 176 |
| Print the on-screen document | 174 |
| Save a document again | 64 |
| Save a document for the first time | 62 |
| Save a document with a new name | 66 |
| Save and close a document | 68 |
| Save selected text | 78 |
| Save the primary file | 196 |
| Save the secondary file | 190 |
| Search and replace text | 118 |
| Search for text | 116 |
| Select a menu command | 28 |
| Select a printer | 168 |
| Select text | 48 |
| Set margins | 140 |
| Set tabs | 136 |
| Start WordPerfect for Windows | 26 |
| Undelete text | 52 |
| Underline text | 104 |
| Use the thesaurus | 124 |
| Use Undo | 58 |

# Entering and Editing Text

This section includes the following tasks:

Start WordPerfect for Windows
Select a menu command
Exit WordPerfect for Windows
Get help
Add text
Overwrite text
Insert a blank line
Combine paragraphs
Insert a tab
Enter a page break
Go to a page
Select text
Delete text
Undelete text
Copy text
Move text
Use Undo

# TASK

## Start WordPerfect for Windows

before

**Oops!**
Be sure to double-click the mouse. If nothing happens or if the icon slides around, you might have paused too long between clicks or moved the mouse between clicks. Try double-clicking again.

1. Turn on the computer and monitor.

   Every computer has a different location for its power switch. Check the side, the front, and the back of your computer. Your monitor also might have a separate power switch. If so, turn on this switch, also.

2. If necessary, respond to the prompts for date and time.

   Some systems ask you to enter the current date and time. (Many of the newer models enter the time and date automatically. If you aren't prompted for these entries, don't worry.)

   If you are prompted, type the current date and press Enter. Then type the current time and press Enter.

3. Type **win** and press **Enter**.

   Win is the command to start Windows. The Program Manager appears on-screen. The Program Manager is an application that comes with Microsoft Windows.

4. Double-click on the group icon for WordPerfect for Windows.

   To double-click, click the mouse button twice in rapid succession. This step opens the WordPerfect for Windows program group. In Windows, programs are stored in group windows. If the window is already open, you can skip this step.

**after**

5. Double-click on the program icon for WordPerfect for Windows.

   This step starts the WordPerfect for Windows program. A blank document appears on-screen.

   Your screen might also include a Button Bar and Ruler across the top of the screen. Do not worry. You can decide whether you want the Button Bar and Ruler to appear on-screen, and you can choose to either hide or display these elements (see *TASK: Display the Button Bar* and *TASK: Display the Ruler*).

**Exit WordPerfect for Windows**
To exit WordPerfect for Windows, see *TASK: Exit WordPerfect for Windows*.

# REVIEW

# To start WordPerfect for Windows

1. Turn on your computer and monitor.
2. Respond to the prompts for the date and time, if necessary.
3. Type **win** and press **Enter**.
4. Double-click on the group icon for WordPerfect for Windows.
5. Double-click on the program icon for WordPerfect for Windows.

**Install WordPerfect**
To start WordPerfect for Windows, the program must be installed. Follow the installation procedures outlined in the WordPerfect for Windows manual.

Entering and Editing Text

27

# TASK

## Select a menu command

**before**

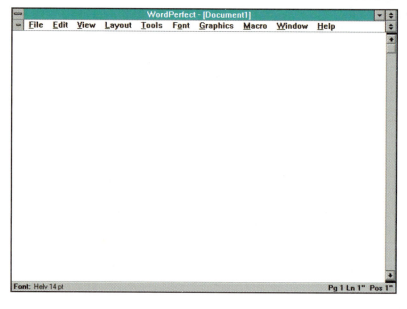

**Oops!**
To close a menu without making a selection, click on the menu heading again or press the Esc key.

1. Point to **File** in the menu bar and click the left mouse button.

   This step opens the File menu. You see a list of File commands. The After screen shows this step.

2. Click on **Exit**.

   This step executes the command. In this case, the step chooses the Exit command. You return to the Windows Program Manager.

   To get back to WordPerfect, double-click on the WordPerfect for Windows group icon. Then double-click on the WordPerfect for Windows program icon.

*Easy* WordPerfect for Windows

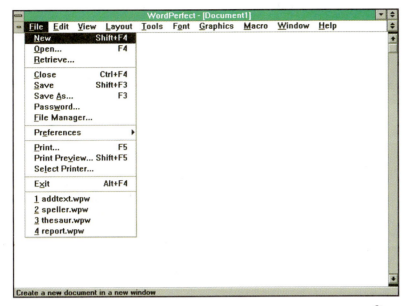

**after**

1. Click on the name of the menu you want to open.
2. Click on the command you want to execute.

**Commands followed by arrows?**
When a command is followed by an arrow, selecting that command will display another menu (called a *cascading menu*). To select a command from the second menu, click on the command.

### REVIEW

# To select a menu command

**Commands with ellipses (...)?**
When a command is followed by an ellipsis, selecting that command will display a dialog box. The dialog box prompts you for additional information.

Entering and Editing Text

29

# TASK

## Exit WordPerfect for Windows

**Oops!**
To restart WordPerfect for Windows, see *TASK: Start WordPerfect for Windows.*

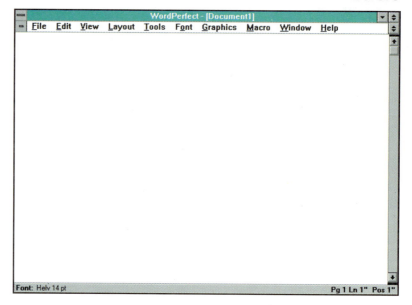

before

1. Point to **File** in the menu bar and click the left mouse button.

   This step opens the File menu. You see a list of File commands.

2. Click on **Exit**.

   This step chooses the Exit command. You return to the Windows Program Manager.

   If you only want to exit WordPerfect for Windows, you can stop here. If, however, you also want to exit Microsoft Windows and return to DOS, follow steps 3 through 5. The After screen shows how the screen looks when you return to DOS.

3. Click on **File** in the Program Manager menu bar.

   This step opens the File menu for the Program Manager of Microsoft Windows.

4. Click on **Exit Windows**.

   This step selects the Exit Windows command. The Exit Windows dialog box appears on-screen.

5. Click on **OK**.

   This step confirms that you want to exit. You return to DOS and the DOS `C:\>` prompt appears on-screen.

after

**Save your document**
If you have typed any text or made any changes to the document, you are prompted to save the changes. See any of the tasks on saving a document in the section "Working with Files."

## REVIEW

1. Click on **File** in the menu bar.
2. Click on the **Exit** command.

   To exit Microsoft Windows, follow steps 3 through 5.

3. Click on **File** in the menu bar.
4. Click on the **Exit Windows** command.
5. Click on the **OK** button.

# To exit WordPerfect for Windows

**Try a shortcut**
Press the Alt+F4 key combination to select the File Exit command.

Entering and Editing Text

# TASK

## Get help

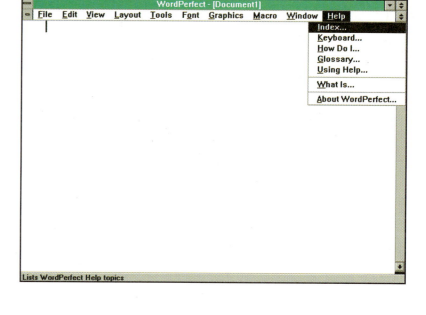

before

**Oops!**
To close the Help window, double-click on the Control menu icon for the Help window (the hyphen or little box in the upper left corner of the window).

1. Point to **Help** in the menu bar and click the left mouse button.

   This step opens the Help menu. On-screen, you see a list of Help menu options.

2. Click on **How Do I**.

   This step selects the How Do I command. The Help window opens, and the name of the Help window appears in the title bar of the Help menu.

3. Click on **Edit**.

   When the mouse pointer is on a topic for which you can get help, the pointer changes to a hand with a pointing finger.

   This step displays Edit topics.

4. Click on **Cancel**.

   This step displays help on the selected topic. In this case, you see an explanation of how to use Undo. (The After screen shows this step.) You can scroll this window by clicking on the scroll arrows. After you read the explanation, close the Help window by following steps 5 and 6.

*Easy* **WordPerfect for Windows**

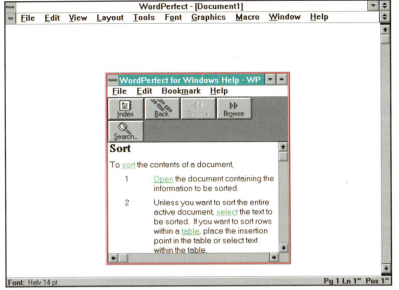

after

5. Click on **File**.

    This step opens the File menu. Be sure to click on the File menu within the Help window.

6. Click on **Exit**.

    This step selects the Exit command and closes the Help window.

**Need more help?**
WordPerfect offers many ways to get help, and the Help feature has its own menu system. For complete information on all Help options, see *Using WordPerfect 5.2 for Windows*, Special Edition.

# REVIEW

## To get help

1. Click on **Help** in the menu bar.
2. Click on the **How Do I** command.
3. Click on the category you want.
4. Click on the topic you want.
5. To close Help, click on **File** in the Help menu bar.
6. Click on the **Exit** command.

Entering and Editing Text

# TASK

## Add text

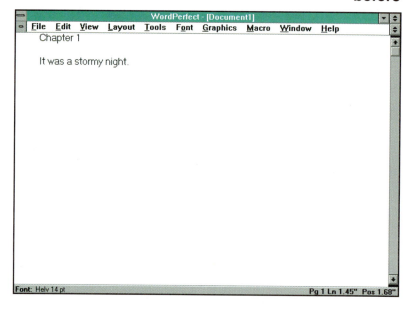

before

**Oops!**
To remove text, select Undo from the Edit menu immediately after typing the new text. You also can delete text. See *TASK: Delete text*.

1. **Type the text in the Before screen.**
   This step gets you ready to add text. Remember that to accomplish the tasks in this book, you must first type any text that appears in the Before screen.

2. **Click before the word *stormy*.**
   This step places the insertion point where you want to insert text. You also can move the insertion point by using the arrow keys.

3. **Type dark and.**
   The new text is inserted and pushes existing text right.

4. **Press the space bar once.**
   This step inserts a space between the new text and the original text.

*Easy* WordPerfect for Windows

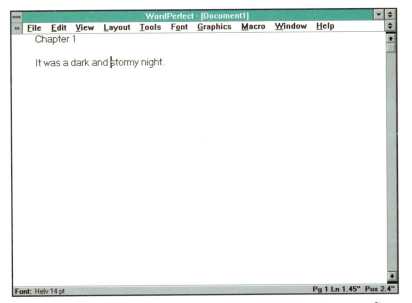

after

**Overwrite text**
You do not press the Ins key to insert text. Pressing the Ins key places WordPerfect in Typeover mode. For more information, see *TASK: Overwrite text*.

# REVIEW

## To add text

1. Place the insertion point where you want to insert new text.

2. Type the text.

3. If necessary, insert a space.

# TASK

## Overwrite text

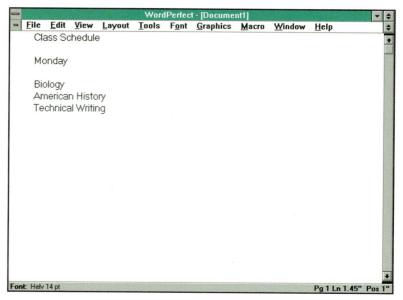
before

**Oops!**
To reverse the change, select Undo from the Edit menu immediately after you overtype the text.

1. Click before the *M* in *Monday*.

   This step places the insertion point where you want to insert text. You can place the insertion point by clicking the mouse button or by using the arrow keys.

2. Press **Ins**.

   Pressing the Ins key places WordPerfect in Typeover mode. The word `Typeover` appears in the status bar. This mode overwrites text rather than inserts text.

3. Type **Fri**.

   The original text is deleted and replaced with *Fri*.

4. Press **Ins**.

   The Ins key is a toggle. Pressing it once turns on Typeover mode. Pressing it again turns off Typeover mode.

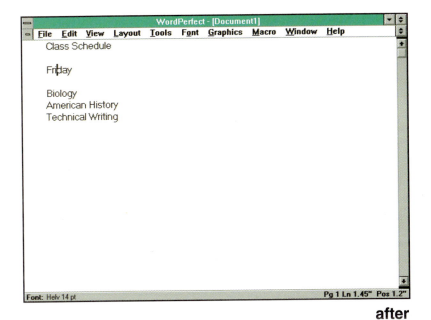

after

**Use another method**
You also can select the text you want to replace and start typing. The new text will replace the selected text. This method saves you from having to select, then delete, and then type the text.

## REVIEW

## To overwrite text

1. Place the insertion point where you want to start overwriting text.

2. Press **Ins**.

3. Type the new text.

4. Press **Ins** again.

Entering and Editing Text

37

# TASK

## Insert a blank line

**Oops!**
To delete the blank line, see *TASK: Combine paragraphs*.

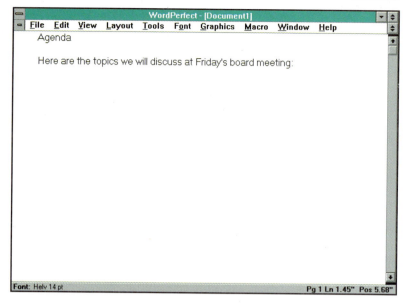

before

1. Click after *meeting:*.
   Be sure to click after the colon at the end of the sentence. This step places the insertion point where you want to insert a blank line.

2. Press **Enter once**.
   This step ends the current line. When you press Enter, WordPerfect inserts a hard return code—[HRt]—into the document.

3. Press **Enter** again.
   This step inserts a new, blank line.

4. Type **Scheduled projects**.
   Notice that a blank line separates the original text and the new text.

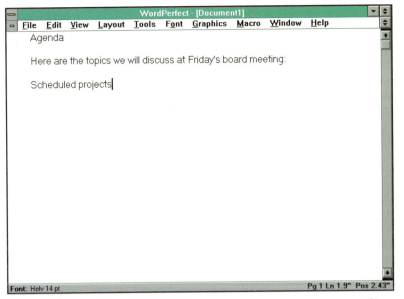

**after**

**What is word wrap?**
Unlike a typewriter, you don't have to press Enter at the end of each line of text. When text reaches the end of the line, WordPerfect automatically moves the text to the next line. This feature is called *word wrap*.

## REVIEW

## To insert a blank line

1. Move the insertion point to the end of the paragraph.
2. Press **Enter twice**.

**Hard return vs. soft return**
A hard return forces a line break. If you add or delete text, the hard return stays in the same spot in the text. WordPerfect automatically inserts a soft return. When you add or delete text, the soft returns are adjusted. In this exercise, you created a hard return.

**Entering and Editing Text**

# TASK

## Combine paragraphs

before

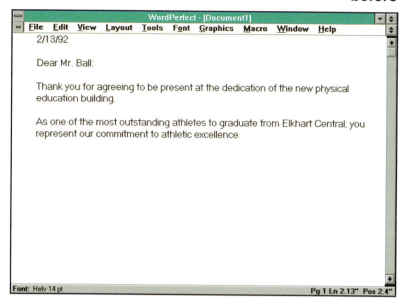

**Oops!**
To split the paragraphs and insert a blank line, move the insertion point to where you want the break. Then press Enter twice.

1. Click after *building*.

   Be sure to click after the period. This step places the insertion point at the end of the first paragraph.

2. Press **Del once**.

   Pressing the Del key deletes the blank line between the two paragraphs.

3. Press **Del** again.

   This step deletes the end-of-paragraph return. The second paragraph moves up next to the first paragraph.

4. Press the **space bar once**.

   Pressing the space bar inserts a space between the two sentences.

*Easy* **WordPerfect for Windows**

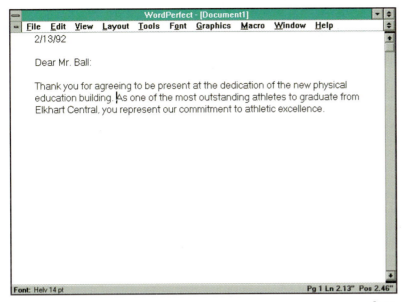

after

## REVIEW

## To combine paragraphs

1. Move the insertion point to the end of the last line in the first paragraph.

2. Press **Del** to delete the hard return at the end of the paragraph. If there is a blank line between the paragraphs, press **Del twice**.

3. Press the **space bar**.

Entering and Editing Text

# TASK

## Insert a tab

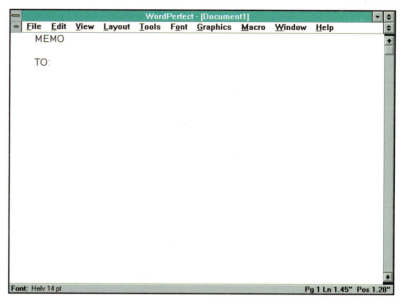
before

**Oops!**
To delete the tab, click after the tab and press the Backspace key.

1. Click after *To:*.
   This step places the insertion point where you want to insert a tab. Be sure to click after the colon.

2. Press **Tab**.
   Pressing the Tab key inserts a tab and moves the insertion point to the next tab stop. WordPerfect default tabs are set every half inch. You can change the tab settings. See *TASK: Set tabs*.

3. Type **All employees**.
   The text you type begins at the location of the tab stop.

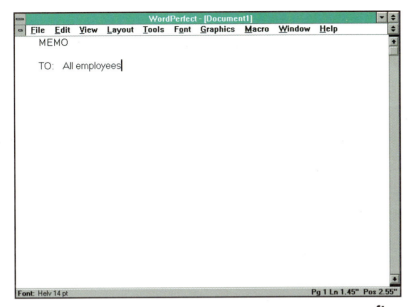

after

1. Place the insertion point where you want to insert the tab.
2. Press **Tab**.

**Indent text**
To indent an entire paragraph from the left margin, use the Indent command. See *TASK: Indent text*.

### REVIEW

# To insert a tab

Entering and Editing Text

# TASK

## Enter a page break

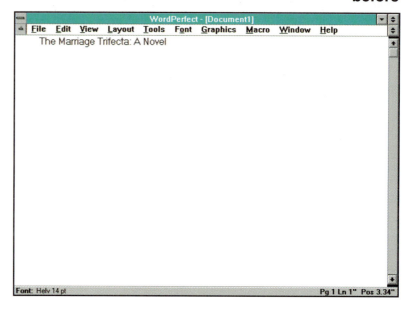

before

### Oops!
To delete the page break, select Undo from the Edit menu immediately after inserting the page break. Or press the Alt+F3 key combination to turn on Reveal Codes; delete the [HPg] code.

1. **Click after the word *Novel*.**

   This step places the insertion point where you want the new page to begin. Remember that you can use the mouse or the arrow keys to position the insertion point.

2. **Click on Layout in the menu bar.**

   This step opens the Layout menu. You see a list of Layout commands.

3. **Click on Page.**

   This step selects the Page command. You see a list of Page options.

4. **Click on Page Break.**

   This step inserts a hard page break into your document. On-screen, you see a double line. When you print the document, a new page will begin where you inserted the page break.

*Easy* **WordPerfect for Windows**

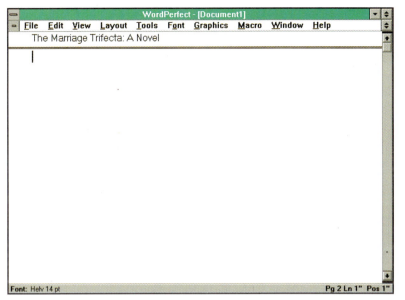

after

**Try a shortcut**
Press the Ctrl+Enter key combination to enter a hard page break.

---

### REVIEW

1. Place the insertion point where you want the new page to begin.
2. Click on **Layout** in the menu bar.
3. Click on the **Page** command.
4. Click on the **Page Break** command.

## To enter a page break

**Hard page break vs. soft page break**
You insert a hard page break manually. When you make changes to a document, the page break remains in the same spot. WordPerfect automatically inserts a soft page break. When you add or delete text, the soft page breaks are adjusted automatically. A soft page break appears as a single dashed line on-screen.

Entering and Editing Text

45

## TASK

# Go to a page

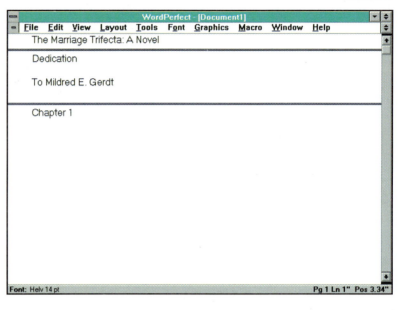
before

**Oops!**
To move back to the original insertion point, select Go To and click on the Last Position button. You cannot use the Edit Undo command to reverse the movement.

1. **Click after the word *Novel*.**

   This step places the insertion point on the first page of a three-page document. You also can use the arrow keys to position the mouse pointer.

2. **Click on Edit in the menu bar.**

   This step opens the Edit menu. You see a list of Edit commands.

3. **Click on Go To.**

   This step selects the Go To command. The Go To dialog box appears. The insertion point is located inside the Go To Page Number text box. The current page number is listed in this box.

4. **Type 3.**

   Typing 3 tells WordPerfect to go to page 3.

5. **Click on OK.**

   This step confirms the command. WordPerfect moves the insertion point to page 3. The document window is scrolled so that you see the first line of page 3 at the top of the window.

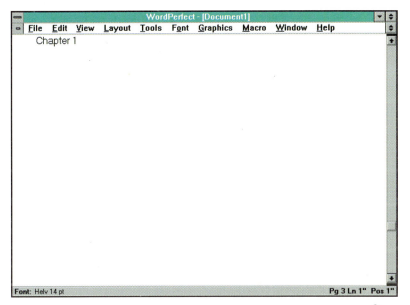

**after**

**Move to the top of the document**
To move to the top of the document, press the Ctrl+Home key combination.

# REVIEW

1. Click on **Edit** in the menu bar.
2. Click on the **Go To** command.
3. Type the page number in the Go To Page Number text box.
4. Click on the **OK** button.

## To go to a page

**Try a shortcut**
Press the Ctrl+G key combination to select the Go To command.

**Entering and Editing Text**

# TASK

## Select text

**before**

**Oops!**
To deselect text, click outside the selected text.

1. Click before the *I* in *It*.

   This step places the insertion point where you want to start selecting text. You also can use the arrow keys to position the insertion point.

2. Hold down the mouse button and drag the mouse pointer across the text until you highlight the sentence *It was a dark and stormy night*.

   This step selects the text. While you continue to hold down the mouse button, you can extend the selection. `Select On` appears in the status bar.

3. Release the mouse button.

   The selected text appears in reverse video on-screen. After you select text, you can make many changes to the text— delete it, copy it, move it, make it bold, and so on. See the other tasks in this book.

   You also can use the menus to select text. Place the insertion point in the sentence or paragraph you want to select. To select a sentence, from the Edit menu, click on Select and then click on Sentence. To select a paragraph, from the Edit menu, click on Select and then click on Paragraph.

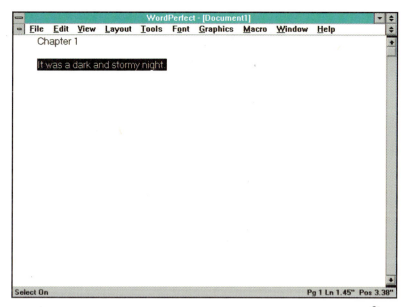

**after**

1. Click at the start of the text you want to select.

2. Hold down the mouse button and drag across the text you want to select.

3. Release the mouse button.

**Select text by using the keyboard**
To select text by using the keyboard, place the insertion point where you want to start selecting text. Then hold down the Shift key and use the arrow keys to highlight the text.

# REVIEW

# To select text

**Try a shortcut**
To select text quickly, place the insertion point in the word, sentence, or paragraph you want to select. Then double-click the mouse to select a word. Triple-click to select a sentence. Quadruple-click to select a paragraph.

# TASK

## Delete text

**before**

**Oops!**
To restore the deleted text, select Undo from the Edit menu. Or select Undelete from the Edit menu. See *TASK: Use Undo* and *TASK: Undelete text* for more information.

1. Click before the *d* in *dark*.

   This step places the insertion point before the text you want to delete. You also can use the arrow keys to position the insertion point.

2. Select the words *dark and*; be sure to select the space after the word *and*.

   You can use either the mouse or the keyboard to select text. To use the mouse, hold down the mouse button, drag across the text you want to select, and then release the mouse button. To use the keyboard, hold down the Shift key and use the arrow keys to select the text. See *TASK: Select text* for more information.

3. Press **Del**.

   Pressing the Del key deletes the selected text. The remaining text moves over to fill in the gap.

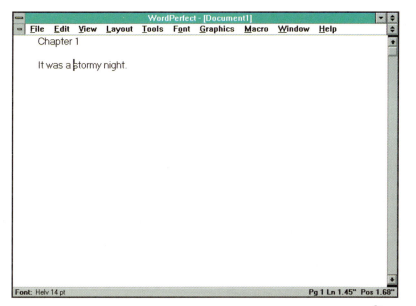

**after**

**Delete a character**
To delete just one character, use the Del or Backspace key. Del deletes the character to the right of the insertion point; Backspace deletes the character to the left of the insertion point. To delete a word, place the insertion point in the word and press the Ctrl+Backspace key combination.

# REVIEW

1. Select the text you want to delete.
2. Press **Del**.

## To delete text

# TASK

## Undelete text

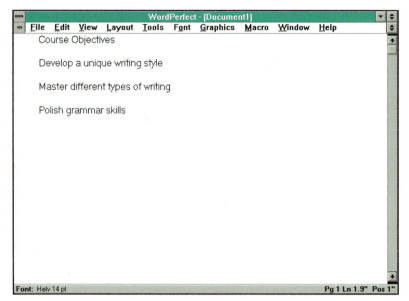

**before**

**Oops!**
To cancel the operation, click on Cancel in step 6 of the Task section. The text remains deleted.

1. Click before the *M* in *Master*.

   This step places the insertion point at the start of the text you want to delete. You also can use the arrow keys to position the mouse pointer. Remember that you must delete text before you can undelete it.

2. Select the entire line and the following blank line.

   You can use either the mouse or the keyboard to select text. To use the mouse, hold down the mouse button, drag across the text you want to select, and then release the mouse button. To use the keyboard, hold down the Shift key and use the arrow keys to select the text. See *TASK: Select text* for more information.

3. Press **Del**.

   Pressing the Del key deletes the selected text.

   If you use the Cut command to delete text, you cannot restore the text with the Undelete command. To restore the text, you would need to use the Paste command.

4. Click on **Edit** in the menu bar.

   This step opens the Edit menu. A list of Edit commands appears.

5. Click on **Undelete**.

   This step selects the Undelete command. The Undelete dialog box appears. You can use this box to cycle through up to three previous deletions. The text you want to restore is the most recent deletion and appears in the document. This text is highlighted.

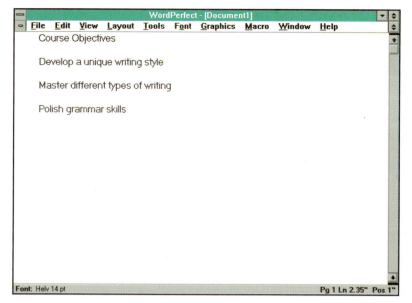

**after**

6. Click on **Restore**.

   This step selects the Restore button and restores the text to the document.

---

**Use Undo**
To restore text, you also can select Undo from the Edit menu. You must use this command immediately after you delete the text. Edit Undo lets you restore only the most recent deletion.

## REVIEW

## To undelete text

1. Click on **Edit** in the menu bar.
2. Click on the **Undelete** command.
3. If necessary, click on **Previous** or **Next** to see the previous or next deletion.
4. When the text you want to restore appears, click on the **Restore** button.

**Try a shortcut**
Press the Alt+Shift+Backspace key combination to select the Edit Undelete command.

**Entering and Editing Text**

# TASK

## Copy text

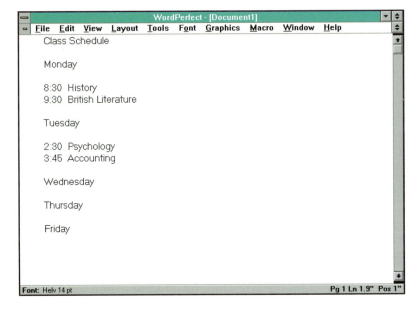

before

**Oops!**
To delete the copied text, select Undo from the Edit menu immediately after pasting the text. You also can simply delete the copied text; see *TASK: Delete text*.

1. Click before the *8* in *8:30*.

   This step places the insertion point at the start of the text you want to copy. You also can use the arrow keys to position the insertion point.

2. Select the next three lines—the line that starts *8:30*, the line that starts *9:30*, and the blank line.

   You can use either the mouse or the keyboard to select text. To use the mouse, hold down the mouse button, drag across the text you want to select, and then release the mouse button. To use the keyboard, hold down the Shift key and use the arrow keys to select the text. See *TASK: Select text* for more information.

   Be sure to select the blank line following the text lines.

3. Click on **Edit** in the menu bar.

   This step opens the Edit menu. A list of Edit commands appears.

4. Click on **Copy**.

   This step selects the Copy command. The text is copied to the Clipboard. (The Clipboard is a temporary holding space for text and graphics.)

5. Click before the *T* in *Thursday*.

   This step places the insertion point where you want the copied text to appear.

54

*Easy* **WordPerfect for Windows**

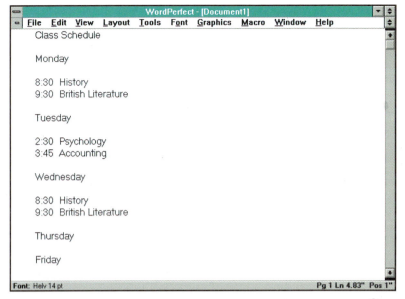

**after**

**Try a shortcut**
Press the Ctrl+Ins key combination to select the Edit Copy command. Press the Shift+Ins key combination to select the Edit Paste command.

6. Click on **Edit** in the menu bar.
   This step opens the Edit menu again. A list of Edit commands appears.

7. Click on **Paste**.
   This step selects the Paste command. The copied text now appears in both locations.

# REVIEW

## To copy text

1. Select the text you want to copy.
2. Click on **Edit** in the menu bar.
3. Click on the **Copy** command.
4. Place the insertion point where you want the copy to appear.
5. Click on **Edit** in the menu bar.
6. Click on the **Paste** command.

**Check formatting**
When you copy or move text, you might have to insert or delete spaces or hard returns to get the text formatted properly.

**Entering and Editing Text**

# TASK

## Move text

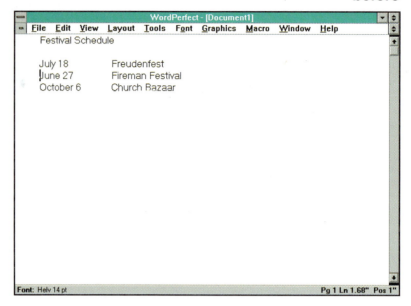

before

**Oops!**
To restore the text to the original location, select Undo from the Edit menu immediately after selecting Paste. Move the insertion point back to the original location and select Paste from the Edit menu.

1. **Click before the *J* in *June*.**

   This step places the insertion point at the start of the text you want to move. You also can use the arrow keys to position the mouse pointer.

2. **Select the entire line of text.**

   You can use either the mouse or the keyboard to select text. To use the mouse, hold down the mouse button, drag across the text you want to select, and then release the mouse button. To use the keyboard, hold down the Shift key and use the arrow keys to select the text. See *TASK: Select text* for more information.

   Be sure to select the entire line (the text and the hard return at the end of the line). The highlight should extend past the text into the margins.

3. **Click on Edit in the menu bar.**

   This step opens the Edit menu. A list of Edit commands appears.

4. **Click on Cut.**

   This step selects the Cut command. The text is cut from the document and placed on the Clipboard (a temporary holding spot).

5. **Click before the *J* in *July*.**

   This step places the insertion point where you want to move the text. You also can use the arrow keys to position text.

*Easy* **WordPerfect for Windows**

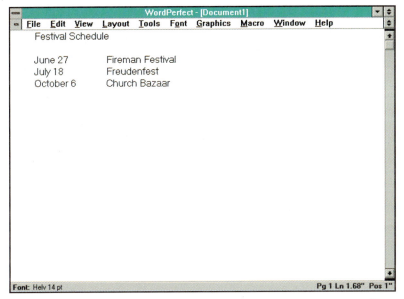

**after**

**Drag and drop**
You can also drag the text to a new location. Select the text. Then click and hold down the mouse button. A shadowed box appears. Drag the text to the new location and release the mouse button.

6. Click on **Edit** in the menu bar.
   This step opens the Edit menu again. A list of Edit menu commands appears.

7. Click on **Paste**.
   This step selects the Paste command. The text is pasted to the new location.

# REVIEW

## To move text

1. Select the text you want to move.
2. Click on **Edit** in the menu bar.
3. Click on the **Cut** command.
4. Place the insertion point where you want the text to appear.
5. Click on **Edit** in the menu bar.
6. Click on the **Paste** command.

**Entering and Editing Text**

**57**

# TASK

## Use Undo

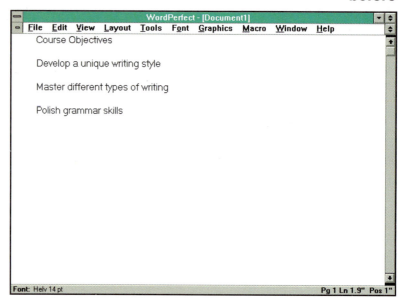

**before**

**Oops!**
To reverse the Undo command, use Edit Undo again.

1. Click before the *M* in *Master*.

   This step places the insertion point at the start of the text you want to delete. You also can use the arrow keys to position the insertion point. In this task, you undo a text deletion, so you will first delete the text so that you can undo the deletion.

2. Select the entire line and the following blank line.

   You can use either the mouse or the keyboard to select text. To use the mouse, hold down the mouse button, drag across the text you want to select, and then release the mouse button. To use the keyboard, hold down the Shift key and use the arrow keys to select the text. See *TASK: Select text* for more information.

3. Press **Del**.

   Pressing the Del key deletes the selected text.

4. Click on **Edit** in the menu bar.

   This step opens the Edit menu. A list of Edit commands appears.

5. Click on **Undo**.

   This step selects the Undo command. The deleted text is restored. (Note that the document window might scroll so that you don't see the first line. The line is still in the document; you just don't see it on-screen. The document window is scrolled in the After screen.)

   You can use Undo for other changes besides restoring deleted text. You can undo copying text, moving text, formatting changes, and so on. You cannot undo merges or scrolling the document.

58

*Easy* **WordPerfect for Windows**

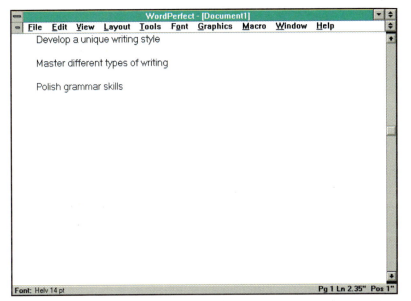
after

**Try a shortcut**
Press the Alt+Backspace key combination to select the Edit Undo command.

---

# REVIEW

1. Click on **Edit** in the menu bar.
2. Click on the **Undo** command.

## To use Undo

**Select Undo immediately**
Undo reverses the *last* change you made to the document. If you make a change you want to undo, you must select Edit Undo immediately.

# Working with Files

This section includes the following tasks:

Save a document for the first time

Save a document again

Save a document with a new name

Save and close a document

Abandon changes

Open a document

Display files in a different directory

Create a new document

Save selected text

Combine two documents

Open more than one document

Display more than one document

Make a different document active

Delete a file

# TASK

## Save a document for the first time

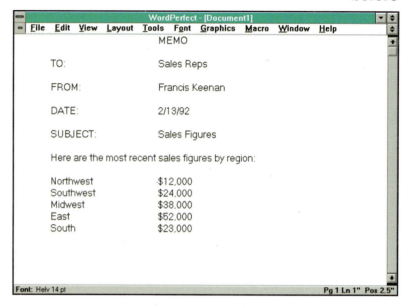

**before**

**Oops!**
If you don't want to save the file, click Cancel for step 4.

1. Click on **File** in the menu bar.

   This step opens the File menu. You see a list of File commands.

2. Click on **Save**.

   This step selects the Save command. When you save the file for the first time, the Save As dialog box appears. This box displays the current directory, two lists (a file list and a directory list), and a text box. The insertion point is positioned in the Save As text box so that you can type a file name.

   For information on the other dialog box options, see *Using WordPerfect 5.2 for Windows,* Special Edition.

3. Type **SALES.MEM**.

   SALES.MEM is the name you want to assign the file. A file name consists of two parts: the file name and the extension. For the file name, you can type up to eight characters. The extension, which can be up to three characters, usually indicates the type of file. A period separates the file name and the extension. As a general rule, use only letters and numbers for file names.

4. Click on **Save**.

   This step confirms the file name. The file is saved to disk and remains on-screen. The name of the file appears in the title bar at the top of the screen. The path (the directory where the document is stored) also appears in the title bar. If you had not made any changes, the word `unmodified` appears after the file name.

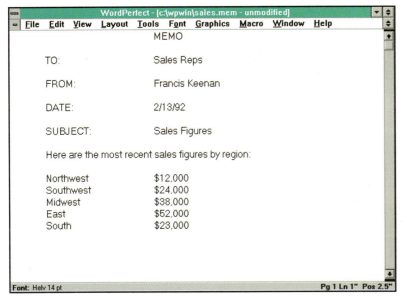
**after**

As a general rule, you should save every 5 to 10 minutes. To save the file again, see *TASK: Save a document again*. Also, save the file before you try a task of which you are unsure.

1. Click on **File** in the menu bar.
2. Click on the **Save** command.
3. Type a file name.
4. Click on the **Save** button.

**File already exists?**
If you type the same name as another file, you see a message box that tells you the file already exists and asks whether you want to replace the file. Click on Yes if you want to replace the file. Otherwise, click on No and save the file with a different name.

### REVIEW

# To save a document for the first time

**Try this shortcut**
You also can press the Shift+F3 key combination to select the File Save command.

**Working with Files**

# TASK

## Save a document again

**before**

```
WordPerfect - [c:\wpwin\sales.mem]
File  Edit  View  Layout  Tools  Font  Graphics  Macro  Window  Help

                        MEMO

        TO:          Sales Reps

        FROM:        Francis Keenan

        DATE:        2/13/92

        SUBJECT:     Sales Figures

        Here are the most recent sales figures by region:

        Northwest           $12,000
        Southwest           $24,000
        Midwest             $38,000
        East                $52,000
        South               $23,000

Font: Helv 14 pt                              Pg 1 Ln 1" Pos 2.5"
```

**Oops!**
If you don't want to save the file, you can abandon any changes you have made. See *TASK: Abandon changes*.

1. Click on **File** in the menu bar.
   This step opens the File menu. A list of File commands appears.

2. Click on **Save**.
   This step selects the Save command. The file is saved with the same file name and remains on-screen. As the file is being saved, you might briefly see a message in the status bar—Saving. After you save the document (and if you make no additional changes), the word unmodified appears after the file name.

**after**

**Save often**
As a general rule, you should save every 5 to 10 minutes. In the event of a power loss, you can lose all your work if you haven't saved your document.

## REVIEW

1. Click on **File** in the menu bar.
2. Click on the **Save** command.

## To save a document again

**Try a shortcut**
Press the Shift+F3 key combination to select the File Save command.

# TASK

## Save a document with a new name

**before**

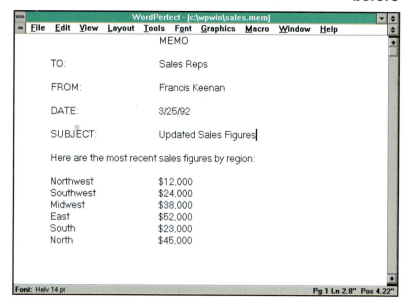

**Oops!**
If you don't want to save the file, click on Cancel for step 4.

1. Click on **File** in the menu bar.

    This step opens the File menu. A list of File commands appears.

2. Click on **Save As**.

    This step selects the Save As command. The File Save As dialog box appears. This box displays the current directory, lists files and directories, and includes the Save As text box. This text box contains the current file name; the file name is selected.

    For information on the other dialog box options, see *Using WordPerfect 5.2 for Windows,* Special Edition.

3. Type **NEWSALES.MEM**.

    NEWSALES.MEM is the new name you want to assign the file. A file name consists of two parts: the file name and the extension. For the file name, you can type up to eight characters. The extension, which can be up to three characters and is optional, usually indicates the type of file. A period separates the file name and the extension. As a general rule, use only letters and numbers for file names.

4. Click on **Save**.

    This step confirms the file name. WordPerfect saves the file to disk with the new name, and the new file remains on-screen. The new name appears in the title bar. The original document remains intact on disk.

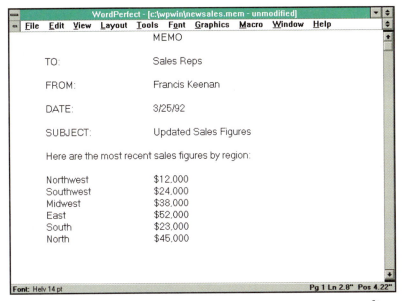

after

1. Click on **File** in the menu bar.
2. Click on the **Save As** command.
3. Type a file name.
4. Click on the **Save** button.

**File already exists?**
If you type the name of another file, a message box appears to warn you that the file already exists and to ask whether you want to replace the file. Click on Yes if you want to replace the file. Otherwise, click on No and save the file with a different name.

## REVIEW

# To save a document with a new name

**Try a shortcut**
Press the F3 key to select the File Save As command.

# TASK

## Save and close a document

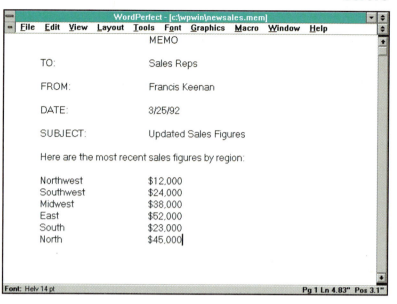

**before**

**Oops!**
To reopen the file that you closed, see *TASK: Open a document*.

1. **Save the document.**

   For help with this step, see any of the tasks on saving a document in this section. For this task, save the document with the name NEWSALES.MEM.

2. **Click on File in the menu bar.**

   This step opens the File menu. A list of File commands appears.

3. **Click on Close.**

   This step selects the Close command. The document closes, and a blank document remains on-screen. A blank document is always open on-screen.

   If you haven't saved the document, WordPerfect asks whether you want to save it. Click on Yes to save the document; click on No to close without saving.

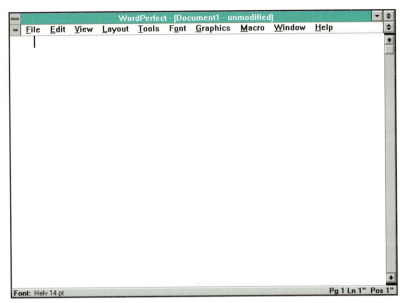
**after**

**Try a shortcut**
Press the Ctrl+F4 key combination to select the File Close command.

---

# REVIEW

1. Save the document.
2. Click on **File** in the menu bar.
3. Click on the **Close** command.

## To save and close a document

Working with Files

# TASK

## Abandon changes

*before*

**Oops!**
If you want to save the file, click on Yes in step 3, and then save the document. You also can click on Cancel in step 3 to return to the document.

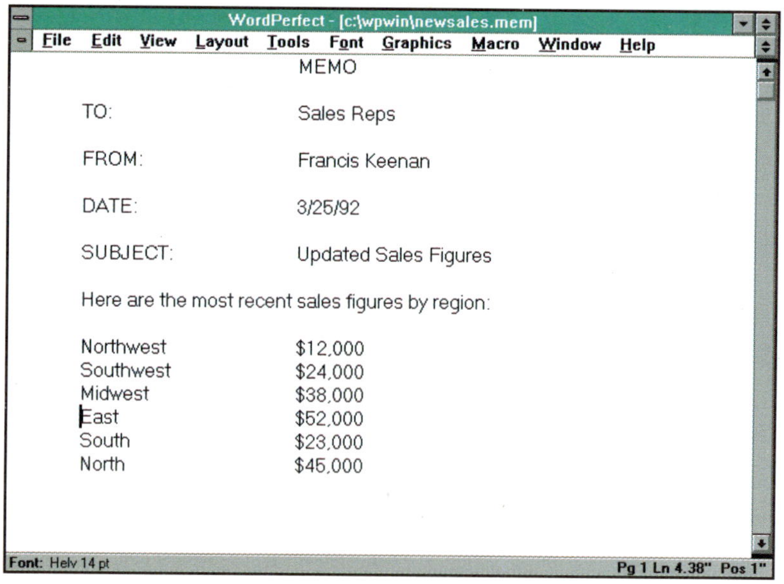

1. Click on **File** in the menu bar.

   This step opens the File menu. A list of File commands appears.

2. Click on **Close**.

   This step selects the Close command. If you haven't made any changes to the document, the document closes.

   If you have made changes to the document, a message box appears to ask whether you want to save the changes. In this case, you don't want to save your changes.

3. Click on **No**.

   This step closes the document; any changes you have made are not saved.

70

*Easy* WordPerfect for Windows

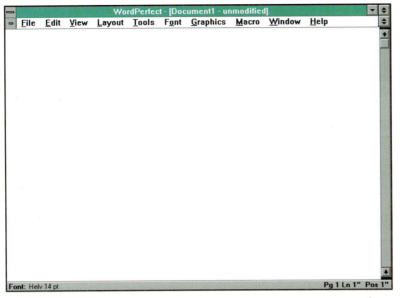

**after**

## REVIEW

1. Click on **File** in the menu bar.
2. Click on the **Close** command.
3. Click on **No**.

## To abandon changes

**Working with Files**

# TASK

## Open a document

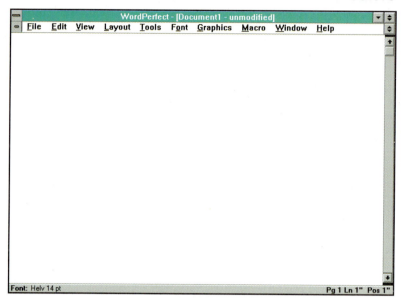

**before**

**Oops!**
If you decide you don't want to open the file, click on Cancel for step 4.

1. Click on **File** in the menu bar.

   This step opens the File menu. A list of File commands appears.

2. Click on **Open**.

   This step selects the Open command. The Open File dialog box appears. This box lists the current directory and includes a list of files, a list of directories, and a Filename text box. The insertion point is positioned in this text box so that you can type the name of the file you want to open.

3. Type **NEWSALES.MEM**.

   NEWSALES.MEM is the name of the file you want to open. You can type the name or click on the name in the file list.

4. Click on **Open**.

   This step selects the Open button; the document appears on-screen. You see the file name in the title bar.

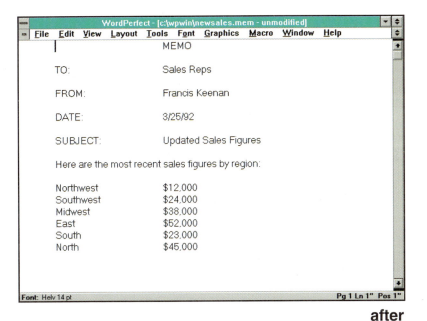

after

**Open a previously opened document**
WordPerfect lists the last four files you had open. To reopen one of these files, click on File in the menu bar. At the bottom of the File menu, click on the name of the file you want.

## REVIEW

1. Click on **File** in the menu bar.
2. Click on the **Open** command.
3. Type or click on the file name you want to open.
4. Click on the **Open** button.

# To open a document

**Try a shortcut**
Press the F4 key to select the File Open command.

Working with Files

73

# TASK

## Display files in a different directory

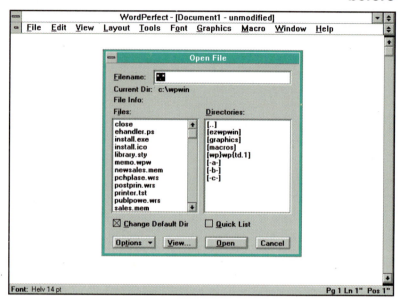

before

**Oops!**
To move back a directory level, double-click on the two-dot entry [..]. This entry represents the parent directory of the current directory. (The parent directory is the directory that contains the current directory.)

1. Click on **File** in the menu bar.

   This step opens the File menu. A list of File commands appears.

2. Click on **Open**.

   This step selects the Open command. The Open File dialog box appears. This box lists the current directory and includes a list of files, a list of directories, and a Filename text box.

   For information on the other dialog box options, see *Using WordPerfect 5.2 for Windows,* Special Edition.

3. Double-click on **[ezwpwin]** in the Directories list.

   Double-click means to press the mouse button twice in rapid succession. This step selects the EZWPWIN directory. (If you don't have this directory, select one you do have.) The files in this directory are now listed in the Files list. You can now open files in this directory.

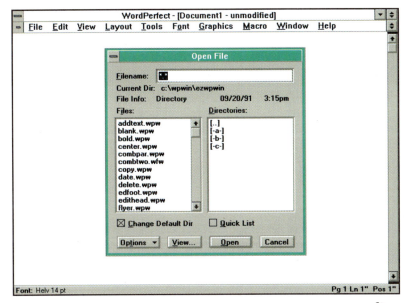

after

**Change drives**
Follow this same procedure to change drives. In the Directories list, click on the drive letter. Click on [-A-], for example, to display files on drive A.

1. Click on **File** in the menu bar.
2. Click on the **Open** command.
3. In the Directories list, double-click on the directory you want.

# REVIEW

# To display files in a different directory

# TASK

## Create a new document

**before**

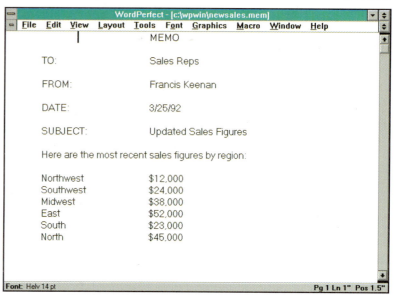

**Oops!**
If you don't want to create a new document, abandon the document. See *TASK: Abandon changes*.

1. Click on **File** in the menu bar.

   This step opens the File menu. A list of File commands appears.

2. Click on **New**.

   This step selects the New command. A new document opens on-screen. `Document2` appears in the title bar. (The number 2 might be different, depending on how many new documents you have created during this WordPerfect session.)

   When you start WordPerfect for the first time, a blank document opens automatically. If you close all open documents, a blank document still remains. WordPerfect always displays at least one blank document. You can use File New to create another empty document window at any time.

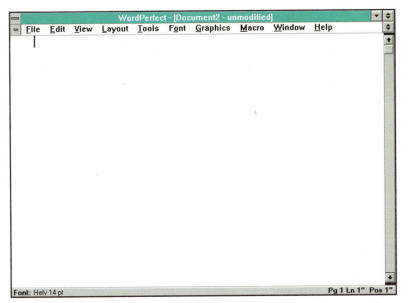

**after**

**Try a shortcut**
Press the Shift+F4 key combination to select the File New command.

## REVIEW

1. Click on **File** in the menu bar.
2. Click on the **New** command.

## To create a new document

# TASK

## Save selected text

**before**

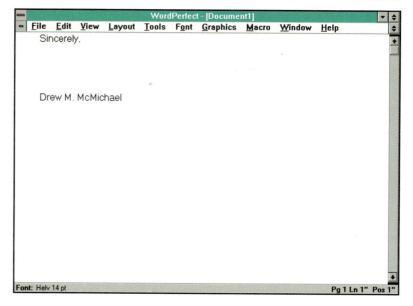

**Oops!**
If you decide you don't want to save the selected text, click on Cancel for step 6 of the Task section.

1. Click before the *S* in *Sincerely*.

   This step places the insertion point at the start of the text you want to save.

2. Select six lines—*Sincerely*, four blank lines, and *Drew M. McMichael*.

   You can use either the mouse or the keyboard to select text. To use the mouse, hold down the mouse button, drag across the text you want to select, and then release the mouse button. To use the keyboard, hold down the Shift key and use the arrow keys to select the text. See *TASK: Select text* for more information.

3. Click on **File** in the menu bar.

   This step opens the File menu. A list of File commands appears.

4. Click on **Save**.

   This step selects the Save command. The Save Selected Text dialog box appears. This box lists the current directory, files, and other directories and contains the Save As text box. The insertion point is positioned in the Save As text box.

5. Type **CLOSING**.

   CLOSING is the name you want to assign this block of text.

6. Click on **Save**.

   This step selects the Save button. The selected text is saved in a file on disk. You return to the document, and the text is still selected.

**after**

**Retrieve text**
To retrieve selected text, see *TASK: Combine two documents*.

Notice that just the text is saved—not the document that contains the text. To save the entire document, see *TASK: Save a document for the first time* or *TASK: Save a document again*.

7. Click outside the selected text.
   This step deselects the text.

# REVIEW

## To save selected text

1. Select the text you want to save.
2. Click on **File** in the menu bar.
3. Click on the **Save** command.
4. Type a file name for the text.
5. Click on the **Save** button.

# TASK

## Combine two documents

**before**

**Oops!**
To cancel the command, click on Cancel for step 6 or No for step 7 in the Task section.

1. Click after the last line of the letter.
   This step places the insertion point at the end of the text. You also can use the arrow keys to position the insertion point.

2. Press **Enter twice**.
   Pressing Enter twice ends the current line and inserts a blank line between the body of the letter and the text you are about to insert.

3. Click on **File** in the menu bar.
   This step opens the File menu. A list of File commands appears.

4. Click on **Retrieve**.
   This step selects the Retrieve command. The Retrieve File dialog box appears. Inside this box, you see the current directory, lists of files and directories, and the Filename text box. The insertion point is positioned in the Filename text box.

5. Type **CLOSING**.
   CLOSING is the name of the document that you want to retrieve. You can also click on the file name in the Files list.

6. Click on **Retrieve**.
   This step selects the Retrieve button. A message box appears that asks you to confirm that you want to insert the file into the current document.

7. Click on **Yes**.
   This step confirms the command. The selected file is inserted into the current document.

80                                            *Easy* WordPerfect for Windows

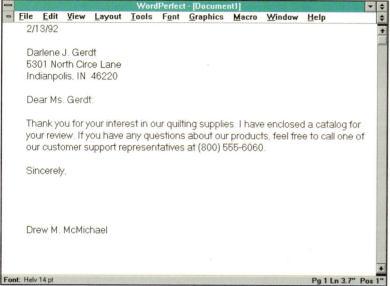

**after**

## File Retrieve vs. File Open

When you select the File Open command, the new document automatically opens in a new, separate window. With File Retrieve, you can insert the document within the current document.

# REVIEW

## To combine two documents

1. Place the insertion point where you want to insert the second document.
2. Click on **File** in the menu bar.
3. Click on the **Retrieve** command.
4. Type the file name you want to retrieve.
5. Click on the **Retrieve** button.
6. Click on **Yes**.

# TASK

## Open more than one document

**before**

*(screenshot of WordPerfect document sales.mem showing a memo to Sales Reps from Francis Keenan, dated 2/13/92, subject: Sales Figures, with regional sales figures: Northwest $12,000; Southwest $24,000; Midwest $38,000; East $52,000; South $23,000)*

**Oops!**
To close a document, see *TASK: Save and close a document.*

1. Click on **File** in the menu bar.

   This step opens the File menu. A list of File commands appears.

2. Click on **Open**.

   This step selects the Open command. The Open File dialog box appears. The insertion point is positioned in the Filename text box.

3. Type **SALES.MEM**.

   SALES.MEM is the name of the file you want to open. If you don't have a file with this name, type the name of one you do have.

4. Click on **Open**.

   This step confirms the command. The selected file appears on-screen. (The Before screen shows this step.) Follow the same steps to open the second document.

5. Click on **File** in the menu bar.

6. Click on **Open**.

7. Type **NEWSALES.MEM**.

   NEWSALES.MEM is the name of the second file you want to open. If you don't have a file with this name, type the name of one you do have.

**after**

**Open many documents**
Depending on the amount of memory your computer has, you can open up to nine documents at once.

8. Click on **Open**.

   This step selects the Open button. The document appears on-screen.

   The first document is still open, but you just cannot see it. To display both documents, see *TASK: Display more than one document*.

# REVIEW

## To open more than one document

1. Click on **File** in the menu bar.
2. Click on the **Open** command.
3. Type the file name or click on the file you want to open.
4. Click on the **Open** button.
5. Click on **File** in the menu bar.
6. Click on the **Open** command.
7. Type the file name or click on the file you want to open.
8. Click on the **Open** button.

# TASK

## Display more than one document

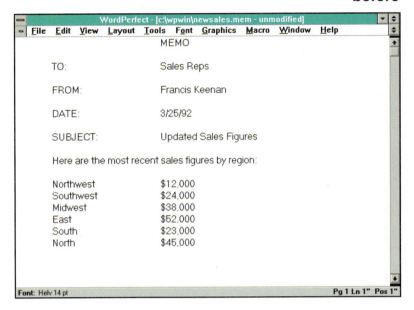

**before**

**Oops!**
To return a document to a full-screen display, move to the document window you want to expand and click on the up arrow in the title bar of that window. (This up arrow is called the Maximize icon.) The window expands to fill the entire screen.

1. Open the documents that you want to display.

   For help with this step, see *TASK: Open more than one document*. For the example, open SALES.MEM and NEWSALES.MEM. If you don't have these two documents, open two documents that you do have.

2. Click on **Window** in the menu bar.

   This step opens the Window menu. A list of Window commands appears. Notice that the bottom of this menu lists the documents that are currently open.

3. Click on **Tile**.

   This step selects the Tile command. Both documents appear in a separate window on-screen. The current or active document (the document that contains the insertion point) has a darker or a colored title bar.

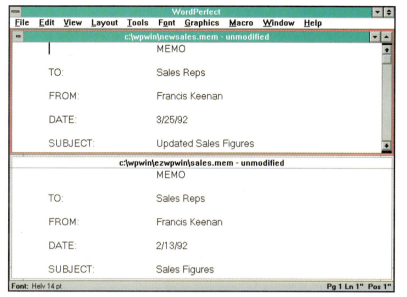

**after**

**Overlap the windows**
You also can make the open windows overlap on-screen. Select the Cascade, rather than Tile, command in step 3.

## REVIEW

## To display more than one document

1. Open the documents that you want to display.
2. Click on **Window** in the menu bar.
3. Click on the **Tile** command.

**Move to a different document**
To make a different document current or active, see *TASK: Make a different document active.*

Working with Files

85

# TASK

## Make a different document active

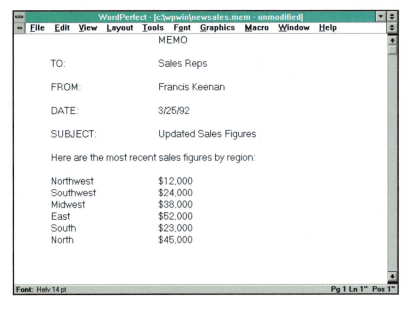

before

**Oops!**
Follow this same procedure to switch to a different document.

1. **Open the documents that you want to use.**

   For help with this step, see *TASK: Open more than one document*. The example uses the documents SALES.MEM and NEWSALES.MEM. If you don't have these documents, open two that you do have. The document that you opened last is the current or active document. In this case, NEWSALES.MEM is the current document.

2. **Click on Window in the menu bar.**

   This step opens the Window menu. A list of Window commands appears. Notice that the bottom of this menu lists the documents that are currently open.

3. **Click on SALES.MEM.**

   This step selects the SALES.MEM document; this document becomes the active (or current) document.

**after**

**Try a shortcut**
If you can see the document—on-screen—that you want to make active, you can click within that document window to make the document active.

## REVIEW

1. Open the documents that you want to use.
2. Click on **Window** in the menu bar.
3. Click on the name of the document that you want to make active.

# To make a different document active

**Working with Files**

**87**

# TASK

## Delete a file

before

**Oops!**
If you decide not to delete the file, click on Cancel for step 4 or step 5 in the Task section.

1. Click on **File** in the menu bar.

   This step opens the File menu. A list of File commands appears.

2. Click on **Open**.

   This step selects the Open command. The Open File dialog box appears. It contains a file list. You use this dialog box to delete files.

3. In the file list, click on the file **SALES.MEM**.

   SALES.MEM is the file you want to delete. You might have to scroll through the list (click on the scroll arrows) to see this file. (You scroll through the list by clicking on the up and down scroll arrows on the side of the list.) The Before screen shows this step.

   If you don't have a file named SALES.MEM, select one you do have. Make sure that you select a file you don't need.

4. Click on the **Options** box; hold down the mouse button and drag down until **Delete** is highlighted, and then release the mouse button.

   This step selects the Delete command. Remember that you must hold down the mouse button to display the commands. You see the Delete File message box. This box prompts you to confirm the deletion.

5. Click on **Delete**.

   This step selects the Delete button and deletes the file. The file is no longer listed in the file list.

*Easy* **WordPerfect for Windows**

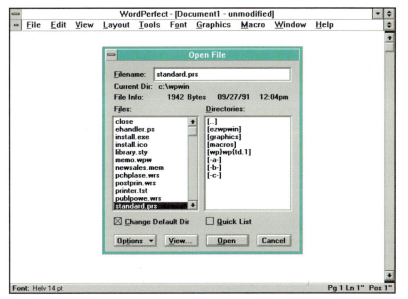

after

**Be careful!**
Be careful when you delete files. Be sure that you don't delete any files that you need. You can only recover deleted files by using a special utility program, such as Norton Utilities.

# REVIEW

## To delete a file

1. Click on **File** in the menu bar.

2. Click on the **Open** command.

3. Click on the name of the file that you want to delete.

4. Click on the **Options** box; hold down the mouse button and drag down until you highlight **Delete**. Then release the mouse button.

5. Click on the **Delete** button.

**Accomplish other file management tasks**
For information on other file management tasks (rename a file, delete a file using another method, and so on), see *Using WordPerfect 5.2 for Windows,* Special Edition.

**Working with Files**

89

# Basic Formatting

This section includes the following tasks:

Display Reveal Codes

Center text

Indent text

Create a hanging indent

Align text flush right

Boldface text

Underline text

Italicize text

Change the font

Change the font size

# TASK

## Display Reveal Codes

**before**

**Oops!**
To return the screen to normal display, select Reveal Codes from the View menu again.

1. Click on **View** in the menu bar.

   This step opens the View menu. You see a list of View commands.

2. Click on **Reveal Codes**.

   This step selects the Reveal Codes command. The insertion point can be anywhere in the text when you select the command.

   The screen is divided horizontally, and the text appears in both windows. The lower part of the screen shows the hidden codes. These codes indicate tabs, margin settings, hard returns, font changes, and so on.

   The insertion point might appear in both screens. When you move the insertion point, it moves in sync in both windows. The insertion point expands when it is on a hidden code, and the entire code is highlighted in the lower half. You can change the formatting of a document by adding or deleting codes. (See the other tasks in this section.)

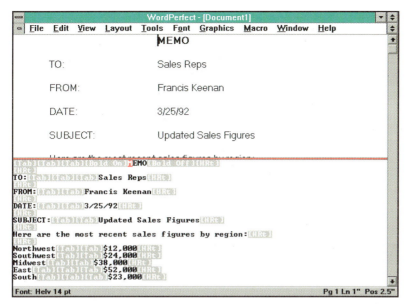

**after**

1. Click on **View** in the menu bar.
2. Click on the **Reveal Codes** command.

**Try a shortcut**
Press the Alt+F3 key combination to select the Reveal Codes command.

# REVIEW

## To display Reveal Codes

**Resize the window**
You can resize the Reveal Codes area by placing the mouse pointer on the bar that separates the windows; the pointer changes to a two-headed arrow. Drag the bar up or down.

**Basic Formatting**

# TASK

## Center text

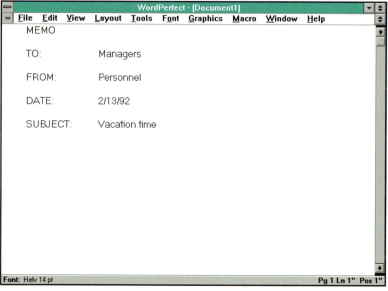

**before**

**Oops!**
To undo the formatting change, select Undo from the Edit menu. Or display Reveal Codes (press the Alt+F3 key combination or select Reveal Codes from the View menu). Then delete the [Center] code.

1. **Click before the *M* in *MEMO*.**
   This step places the insertion point at the beginning of the line you want to center. Be sure that the insertion point is at the beginning of the line.

2. **Click on Layout in the menu bar.**
   This step opens the Layout menu. You see a list of Layout commands.

3. **Click on Line.**
   This step selects the Line command and displays a menu of Line options.

4. **Click on Center.**
   This step selects the Center command; the line is centered on-screen.

94

*Easy* **WordPerfect for Windows**

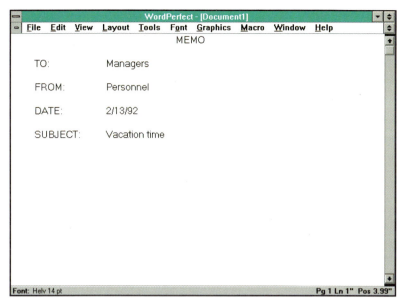

**after**

**Specify centering before you type**
You also can choose to center a line before you type the line. Select the Center command. Then type the text you want to center and press Enter.

# REVIEW

1. Place the insertion point at the beginning of the line you want to center.
2. Click on **Layout** in the menu bar.
3. Click on the **Line** command.
4. Click on the **Center** command.

## To center text

**Try a shortcut**
Press the Shift+F7 key combination to select the Center command.

# TASK

## Indent text

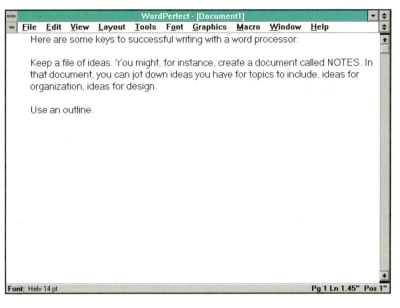

before

**Oops!**
To undo the formatting change, select Undo from the Edit menu. Or display Reveal Codes (press the Alt+F3 key combination or select Reveal Codes from the View menu). Then delete the `[Indent]` code.

1. Click before the *K* in *Keep*.

   This step places the insertion point where you want to indent text. This task indents one paragraph. You can also indent several paragraphs at once. To do so, select the paragraphs for this step. See *TASK: Select text* for more information.

2. Click on **Layout** in the menu bar.

   This step opens the Layout menu. You see a list of Layout commands.

3. Click on **Paragraph**.

   This step selects the Paragraph command. You see a list of paragraph formatting options.

4. Click on **Indent**.

   This step selects the Indent command. The current paragraph is indented from the left margin. The tab settings control how far the text indents. With the default settings, tabs are set every half inch, and the text is indented one half inch.

   You can also indent text from both the left and right margins. To do so, select Double Indent for this step.

**after**

## To indent text

1. Place the insertion point at the beginning of the paragraph you want to indent. To indent several paragraphs, select the paragraphs.

2. Click on **Layout** in the menu bar.

3. Click on the **Paragraph** command.

4. Click on the **Indent** command.

**Try a shortcut**
Press the F7 key to select the Indent command. Press the Ctrl+Shift+F7 key combination to select the Double Indent command.

**REVIEW**

**Specify indenting before you type**
To specify indenting before you type the text to be indented, select the Indent command. Then type the text.

# TASK

## Create a hanging indent

**before**

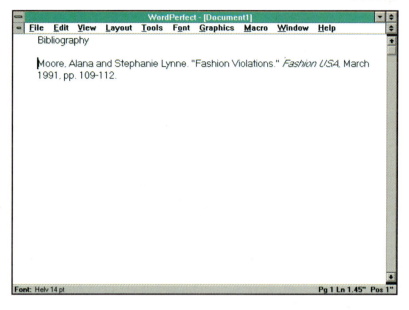

**Oops!**
To undo the formatting change, display Reveal Codes (press the Alt+F3 key combination or select Reveal Codes from the View menu). Then delete the [Indent] and [Mar Rel] codes.

1. Click before the *M* in *Moore*.

   This step places the insertion point where you want to indent text.

   This task creates a hanging indent for one paragraph. You can also make hanging indents for several paragraphs at once. To do so, select the paragraphs for this step. See *TASK: Select text* for more information.

2. Click on **Layout** in the menu bar.

   This step opens the Layout menu. You see a list of Layout commands.

3. Click on **Paragraph**.

   This step selects the Paragraph command. You see a list of paragraph formatting options.

4. Click on **Hanging Indent**.

   This step selects the Hanging Indent command. The first line of the paragraph is flush left, but the second line is indented by one half inch (if you are using the default tab settings).

**after**

**Try a shortcut**
Press the Ctrl+F7 key combination to select the Hanging Indent command.

# REVIEW

1. Place the insertion point at the beginning of the paragraph you want to indent. To indent several paragraphs, select the paragraphs.
2. Click on **Layout** in the menu bar.
3. Click on the **Paragraph** command.
4. Click on the **Hanging Indent** command.

## To create a hanging indent

**Specify a hanging indent before typing**
You can also create hanging indents before you type. To do so, select the Hanging Indent command. Then type your text.

# TASK

## Align text flush right

before

**Oops!**
To undo the formatting change, display Reveal Codes (press the Alt+F3 key combination or select Reveal Codes from the View menu). Then delete the [Flsh Rgt] code.

1. Click before the *S* in *Stephanie*.

   This step places the insertion point at the start of the text you want to align.

2. Select the next three lines of text.

   You can use either the mouse or the keyboard to select text. To use the mouse, hold down the mouse button, drag across the text you want to select, and then release the mouse button. To use the keyboard, hold down the Shift key and use the arrow keys to select the text. See *TASK: Select text* for more information.

   This task aligns several paragraphs. You also can align only one paragraph. To do so, skip this step.

3. Click on **Layout** in the menu bar.

   This step opens the Layout menu. You see a list of Layout commands.

4. Click on **Line**.

   This step selects the Line command. You see a list of line formatting options.

5. Click on **Flush Right**.

   This step selects the Flush Right command. The selected paragraphs are aligned flush with the right margin.

after

**Try a shortcut**
Press the Alt+F7 key combination to select the Flush Right command.

# REVIEW

## To align text flush right

1. Place the insertion point at the beginning of the paragraph you want to align. To align several paragraphs, select the paragraphs.

2. Click on **Layout** in the menu bar.

3. Click on the **Line** command.

4. Click on the **Flush Right** command.

**Specify alignment before typing**
To specify that text should be aligned before you type the text, select the Flush Right command. Then type the text.

**Basic Formatting**

# TASK

## Boldface text

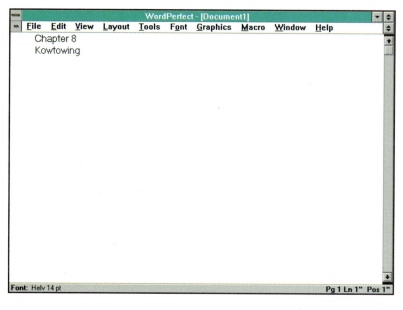

before

**Oops!**
To undo the formatting change, select Undo from the Edit menu immediately. Or display Reveal Codes and delete the [Bold On] code.

1. **Click before the *C* in *Chapter*.**

   This step places the insertion point at the start of the text you want to make bold.

2. **Select the next two lines.**

   You can use either the mouse or the keyboard to select text. To use the mouse, hold down the mouse button, drag across the text you want to select, and then release the mouse button. To use the keyboard, hold down the Shift key and use the arrow keys to select the text. See *TASK: Select text* for more information.

   This task boldfaces several lines of text. You can make any amount of text bold—just select the text you want.

3. **Click on Font in the menu bar.**

   This step opens the Font menu. You see a list of Font commands.

4. **Click on Bold.**

   This step selects the Bold command. The selected text appears in boldface on-screen. (The text is still selected.)

5. **Press →.**

   This step deselects the text. You can press any arrow key or click outside the text to deselect the text.

   When you make text bold, WordPerfect inserts a [Bold On] code at the beginning of the boldface text and a [Bold Off] code at the end. You see these codes only when Reveal Codes is turned on.

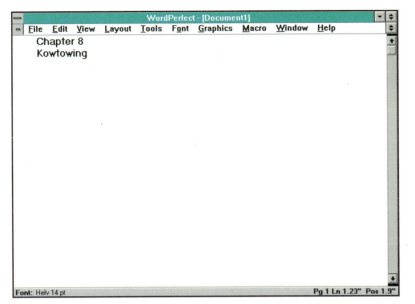

after

**Try a shortcut**
Press the Ctrl+B key combination to select the Bold command.

# REVIEW

## To boldface text

1. Select the text you want to make bold.
2. Click on **Font** in the menu bar.
3. Click on the **Bold** command.
4. Deselect text by pressing any arrow key or clicking outside the selected text.

**Specify boldface before you type**
To specify boldface before you type, select Bold. Type the text, and then press → to move past the [Bold Off] code and return to normal font.

**Basic Formatting**

103

# TASK

## Underline text

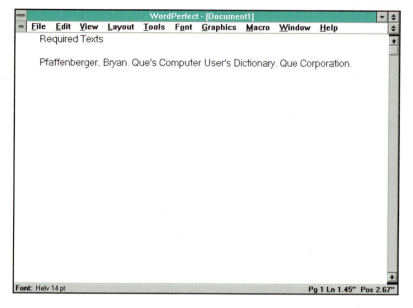

before

**Oops!**
To undo the formatting change, select Undo from the Edit menu immediately. Or display Reveal Codes and delete the [Und On] code.

1. **Click before the *Q* in *Que's*.**

   This step places the insertion point at the start of the text you want to underline.

2. **Select the text *Que's Computer User's Dictionary*.**

   You can use either the mouse or the keyboard to select text. To use the mouse, hold down the mouse button, drag across the text you want to select, and then release the mouse button. To use the keyboard, hold down the Shift key and use the arrow keys to select the text. See *TASK: Select text* for more information.

   This task works on several words. You can underline any amount of text—just select the text to be underlined.

3. **Click on Font in the menu bar.**

   This step opens the Font menu. You see a list of Font commands.

4. **Click on Underline.**

   This step selects the Underline command. The selected text appears underlined on-screen. (The text is still selected.)

5. **Press →.**

   This step deselects the text. You can press any arrow key or click outside the text to deselect the text.

   When you underline text, WordPerfect inserts an [Und on] code at the beginning of the underlined text and an [Und off] code at the end. You see these codes only when Reveal Codes is turned on.

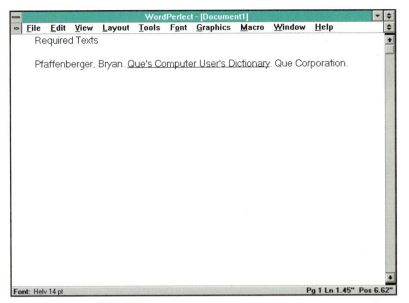

**after**

1. Select the text you want to underline.

2. Click on **Font** in the menu bar.

3. Click on the **Underline** command.

4. Deselect text by pressing any arrow key or clicking outside the selected text.

**Try a shortcut**
Press the Ctrl+U key combination to select the Underline command.

# REVIEW

# To underline text

**Specify underlining before you type**
To specify underlining before you type, select Underline. Type the text, and then press → to move past the [Und Off] code and return to normal font.

**Basic Formatting**

**105**

# TASK

## Italicize text

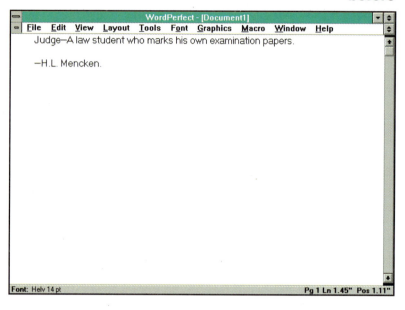

before

**Oops!**
To undo the formatting change, select Undo from the Edit menu immediately. Or display Reveal Codes and delete the `[Italc On]` code.

1. Click before the *H* in *H.L. Mencken*.

   This step places the insertion point at the start of the text you want to italicize.

2. Select the text *H.L. Mencken*.

   You can use either the mouse or the keyboard to select text. To use the mouse, hold down the mouse button, drag across the text you want to select, and then release the mouse button. To use the keyboard, hold down the Shift key and use the arrow keys to select the text. See *TASK: Select text* for more information.

   This task works on several words. You can italicize any amount of text—just select the text to be italicized.

3. Click on **Font** in the menu bar.

   This step opens the Font menu. You see a list of Font commands.

4. Click on **Italic**.

   This step selects the Italic command. The selected text appears in italic on-screen. (The text is still selected.)

5. Press →.

   This step deselects the text. You can press any arrow key or click outside the text to deselect the text.

   When you italicize text, WordPerfect inserts an `[Italc On]` code at the beginning of the italicized text and an `[Italc Off]` code at the end. You see these codes only when Reveal Codes is turned on.

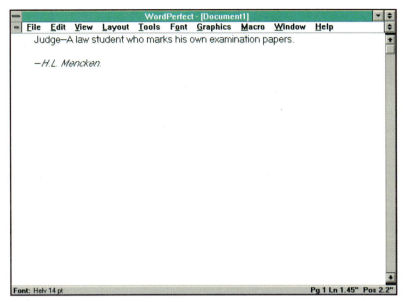

**after**

**Try a shortcut**
Press the Ctrl+I key combination to select the Italic command.

# REVIEW

1. Select the text you want to italicize.

2. Click on **Font** in the menu bar.

3. Click on the **Italic** command.

4. Deselect the text by pressing any arrow key or clicking outside the selected text.

## To italicize text

**Specify italic before you type**
To specify italic before you type, select Italic. Type the text, and then press → to move past the [Italc Off] code and return to normal font.

**TASK**

## Change the font

before

**Oops!**
To undo the formatting change, immediately select Undo from the Edit menu. Or display Reveal Codes and delete the [Font: Tms Rmn 12 pt] code. (The code will vary, depending on the font you selected.)

1. Click before the *A* in *Alana*.

   This step places the insertion point at the start of the text you want to change.

2. Select the next three lines of text.

   You can use either the mouse or the keyboard to select text. To use the mouse, hold down the mouse button, drag across the text you want to select, and then release the mouse button. To use the keyboard, hold down the Shift key and use the arrow keys to select the text. See *TASK: Select text* for more information.

   This task works on several lines. You can change any amount of text—just select the text for which the font will be changed.

3. Click on **Font** in the menu bar.

   This step opens the Font menu. You see a list of Font commands.

4. Click on **Font**.

   This step selects the Font command and displays the Font dialog box. This dialog box lists fonts, point sizes, appearance attributes, and size attributes. The fonts that appear in the dialog box depend on the printer you have set up and selected.

5. In the Font list, click on **Tms Rmn**.

   If you don't have this font, select one you do have. You might have to click on the down scroll arrow to scroll the list and display the font. A sample of the new font appears in the lower left corner of the dialog box.

**after**

6. Click on **OK**.

    This step confirms the new font, and you return to the document. The selected text appears in the new font. (The text is still selected.)

7. Press →.

    This step deselects the text. You can press any arrow key or click outside the text to deselect the text.

**Try a shortcut**
Press the F9 key to open the Font dialog box.

**Change the default font**
You can change the default font for the entire document or for all documents. See *Using WordPerfect 5.2 for Windows*, Special Edition, for complete information on setting preferences.

# REVIEW

# To change the font

1. Select the text you want to change.
2. Click on **Font** in the menu bar.
3. Click on the **Font** command.
4. In the Font list, click on the font you want to use.
5. Click on **OK**.
6. Deselect text by pressing any arrow key or clicking outside the selected text.

**Basic Formatting**

**109**

# TASK

## Change the font size

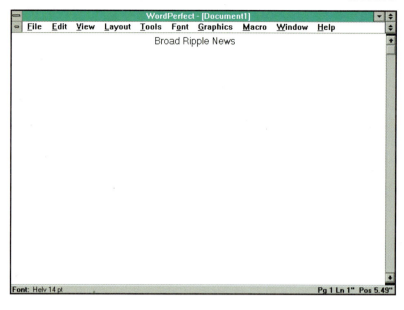

**before**

**Oops!**
To undo the formatting change, display Reveal Codes. Then delete the `[Font: Helv 14 pt]` code. (The code will vary, depending on the font size you selected.)

1. Click before the *B* in *Broad*.

   This step places the insertion point at the start of the text you want to change.

2. Select the text *Broad Ripple News*.

   You can use either the mouse or the keyboard to select text. To use the mouse, hold down the mouse button, drag across the text you want to select, and then release the mouse button. To use the keyboard, hold down the Shift key and use the arrow keys to select the text. See *TASK: Select text* for more information.

   This task changes only one line. You can change any amount of text—just select the text you want to change.

3. Click on **Font** in the menu bar.

   This step opens the Font menu. You see a list of Font commands.

4. Click on **Font**.

   This step selects the Font command and displays the Font dialog box. The current printer, fonts, and point sizes appear. (The fonts that appear depend on the printer you have set up and selected.)

5. In the Point Size list, click on **24**.

   This step selects 24-point type. If you don't have this font size, select one you do have. A sample of the new font appears in the lower left corner of the dialog box.

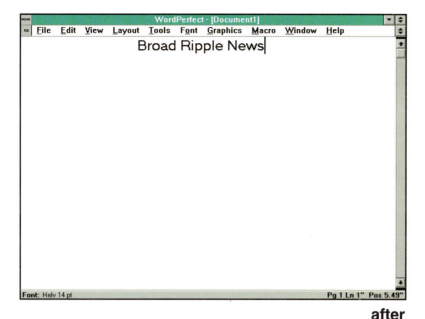

**after**

**Try a shortcut**
Press the F9 key to select the Font command.

6. Click on **OK**.

   This step confirms the new font size, and you return to the document. The selected text appears in the new font size. (The text is still selected.)

7. Press →.

   This step deselects the text. You can press any arrow key or click outside the text to deselect the text.

# REVIEW

## To change the font size

1. Select the text you want to change.
2. Click on **Font** in the menu bar.
3. Click on the **Font** command.
4. In the Font Size list, click on the font size you want to use.
5. Click on the **OK** button.
6. Deselect text by pressing an arrow key or clicking outside the selected text.

**Basic Formatting**

111

# Advanced Editing and Formatting

This section includes the following tasks:

- Insert the date
- Search for text
- Search and replace text
- Check spelling
- Use the thesaurus
- Count words
- Alphabetize text
- Change the case of text
- Display the Ruler
- Display the Button Bar
- Set tabs
- Double-space a document
- Set margins
- Number pages
- Create a header
- Edit a header
- Create a footer
- Edit a footer
- Center a page
- Draw a horizontal line
- Insert a special character
- Insert a graphic
- Move a graphic
- Insert a table
- Enter text into a table

# TASK

## Insert the date

**before**

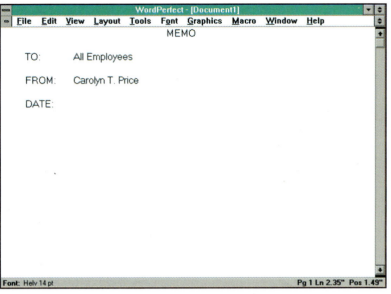

**Oops!**
To delete the date, select Undo from the Edit menu immediately after you insert the date. Or just delete the date. See *TASK: Delete text*.

1. **Click after the word *DATE:*.**
   This step places the insertion point where you will start entering text. Be sure to click after the colon.

2. **Press Tab.**
   Pressing the Tab key inserts a tab so that the text you are about to type will align with the other entries. (You might have to press Tab twice—depending on your tab settings.)

3. **Click on Tools in the menu bar.**
   This step opens the Tools menu. You see a list of Tools commands.

4. **Click on Date.**
   This step selects the Date command. You see a list of Date options.

5. **Click on Text.**
   This step selects the Text command. The current date is inserted into your document, and the insertion point is placed after the date text. (The date that is inserted into your document will differ from the one in the After figure.)

   The default format for dates is Month Day, Year—for instance, October 31, 1991. You also can change the date format with the Date Format command. See *Using WordPerfect 5.2 for Windows, Special Edition*, for more information on this option.

*Easy* **WordPerfect for Windows**

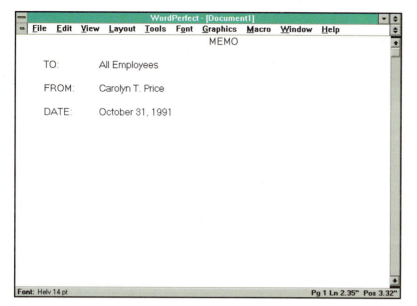

after

**Insert the date code**
Instead of inserting the date text, you can insert a date code into your document. Each time you retrieve the document, the date is updated to the current date. Simply select Code for step 5.

## REVIEW

## To insert the date

1. Place the insertion point where you want to insert the date.
2. Click on **Tools** in the menu bar.
3. Click on the **Date** command.
4. Click on the **Text** command.

**Try a shortcut**
Press the Ctrl+F5 key combination to select the Date Text command.

**Advanced Editing and Formatting**

# TASK

## Search for text

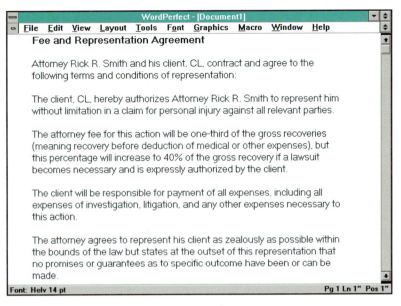

**before**

**Oops!**
If the text isn't found, you see the message `String not found` in the status bar. Try the command again. Double-check that you typed the search string correctly. Also, be sure that the insertion point is at the top of the document when you start the search.

1. **Press Ctrl+Home.**
   Pressing the Ctrl+Home key combination places the insertion point at the top of the document so that you are sure to include all pages in the search. WordPerfect starts searching from the location of the insertion point forward to the end of the document.

2. **Click on Edit in the menu bar.**
   This step opens the Edit menu. You see a list of Edit commands.

3. **Click on Search.**
   This step selects the Search command. You see the Search dialog box. This box includes the Search For text box and other options that control how the document is searched. The insertion point is positioned in the Search For text box.

4. **Type litigation.**
   This text, called the *search string*, is what you want to find. You also can search for codes. See *Using WordPerfect 5.2 for Windows, Special Edition*, for information on this process.

   Be sure to match upper- and lowercase letters exactly. If you type in lowercase only, WordPerfect finds all occurrences. If you type in uppercase only, WordPerfect finds only uppercase matches. For instance, if you type *HARRY*, WordPerfect will not find *Harry*.

   WordPerfect also searches for parts of a word. If you type *the*, for example, WordPerfect stops on *the*, *other*, *theater*, and other words that contain the letters *the*. To search for just the word, insert a space before and after the word in the search string.

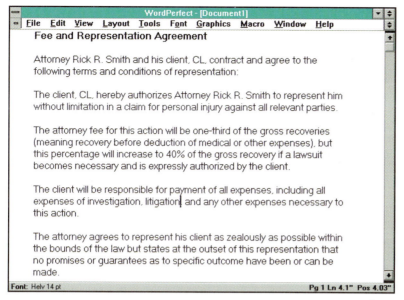

**after**

**Search again**
To search for the next occurrence of the search string, select Search Next from the Edit menu (or press the Shift+F2 key combination).

5. Click on **Search**.

   This step selects the Search button and starts the search. The insertion point moves to the first occurrence of the search string. The insertion point is placed after the text you entered for step 4.

## REVIEW

1. Press **Ctrl**+**Home** to move to the beginning of the document.

2. Click on **Edit** in the menu bar.

3. Click on the **Search** command.

4. Type the text you want to find.

5. Click on the **Search** button to start the search.

# To search for text

**Try a shortcut**
Press the F2 key to select the Search command.

**Advanced Editing and Formatting**

# TASK

## Search and replace text
*(Part 1 of 2)*

**before**

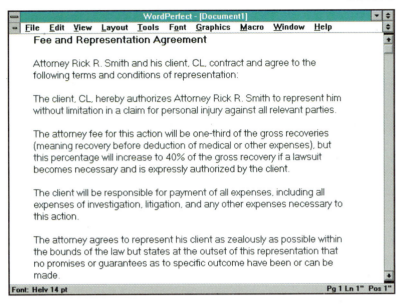

**Oops!**
To cancel the procedure, click on the Close button.

*This task is split into two parts. These two pages contain the first part, Enter the search string. Turn the page for the second part, Replace the text.*

1. Press **Ctrl+Home**.

   Pressing the Ctrl+Home key combination moves the insertion point to the top of the document so that you are sure to include all pages in the search. WordPerfect starts searching from the location of the insertion point forward, to the end of the document.

2. Click on **Edit** in the menu bar.

   This step opens the Edit menu. You see a list of Edit commands.

3. Click on **Replace**.

   This step selects the Replace command. You see the Search and Replace dialog box. The insertion point is positioned in the Search For text box.

4. Type **CL**.

   This text, called the *search string*, is what you want to find. You also can search for codes. (See *Using WordPerfect 5.2 for Windows*, Special Edition, for information on this process.)

5. Click in the **Replace With** text box.

   This step places the insertion point in the Replace With text box so that you can type the replace string.

118

*Easy* **WordPerfect for Windows**

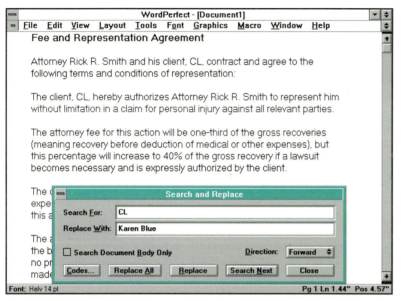

**Try a shortcut**
Press the Ctrl+F2 key combination to select the Replace command

after

6. Type **Karen Blue**.

   This is the text you want to use as the replacement.

## REVIEW

## To search and replace text

1. Press **Ctrl+Home** to move to the beginning of the document.
2. Click on **Edit** in the menu bar.
3. Click on the **Replace** command.
4. Type the text you want to replace.
5. Click in the **Replace With** text box.
6. Type the text you want to use as the replacement.

Advanced Editing and Formatting

# TASK

## Search and replace text
*(Part 2 of 2)*

**Oops!**
To undo the replacements, select Undo from the Edit menu.

before

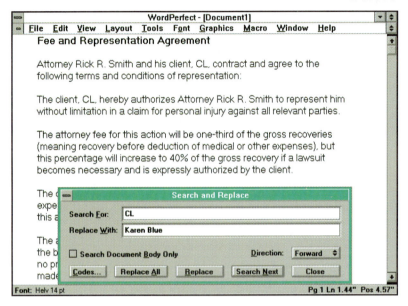

*This task is split into two parts. The preceding two pages contain the first part, Enter the search string. These two pages contain the second part, Replace the text.*

1. Click on **Search Next**.

   This step selects the Search Next button and starts the search. The insertion point moves to the first occurrence of the search string, the text is selected, and the Search and Replace dialog box remains open on-screen.

2. Click on **Replace**.

   This step selects the Replace button. The found text is replaced with the new text. WordPerfect moves to the next occurrence and displays the Search and Replace dialog box.

3. Click on **Replace**.

   This step selects the Replace button and replaces the next occurrence of the text.

4. Click on **Close**.

   This step selects the Close button and closes the dialog box.

120

*Easy* WordPerfect for Windows

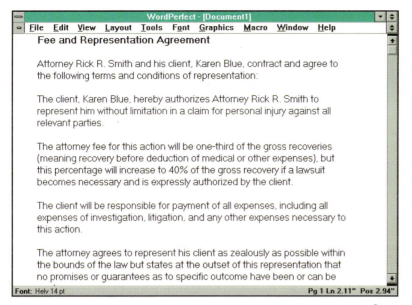

**after**

1. Click on **Search Next** to start the search.

2. Click on the **Replace** button to replace the selected text. Click on the **Replace All** button to make all replacements.

3. Click on the **Close** button to close the dialog box.

**Text not found?**
If the text isn't found, you see the message String not found in the status bar. Try the procedure again and double-check that you typed the search string correctly. Also, be sure that the insertion point is located at the top of the document when you start the search.

## REVIEW

# To search and replace text

**Use the Replace All command**
If you want to make all replacements automatically, select Replace All rather than Replace. Before you select this option, be sure that you want to replace all occurrences of the search string.

# TASK

## Check spelling

**Oops!**
To stop a spelling check, click on Close when WordPerfect stops on a word.

before

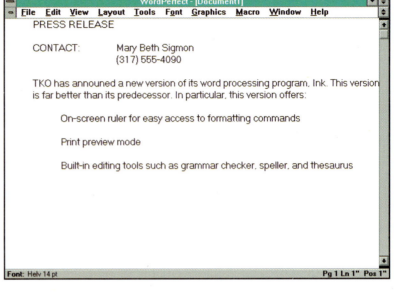

1. Click on **Tools** in the menu bar.

   This step opens the Tools menu. You see a list of Tools commands.

2. Click on **Speller**.

   This step selects the Speller command. You see the Speller dialog box. This dialog box enables you to control how the spelling check is performed. You can use the menu options to specify what to check, what dictionary to use, and other options.

   For this task, the default settings are appropriate.

3. Click on **Start**.

   This step selects the Start button and starts the spelling check. The Speller compares the words in your document to the words in its dictionary and stops on words it cannot find.

   For this example, WordPerfect begins the spelling check and stops on the word *Sigmon*. The word appears at the bottom of the Speller dialog box.

4. Click on **Skip Always**.

   This option tells WordPerfect to skip all occurrences of this word; this word is spelled correctly. WordPerfect continues the spelling check and stops on the word *announed*.

   The correct spelling—announced—appears in the list of suggestions and also in the Replace With text box.

5. Click on **Replace**.

   This step replaces the incorrect spelling with the selected spelling. (If the correct spelling is not selected, click on it in the suggestion list; then click on Replace.)

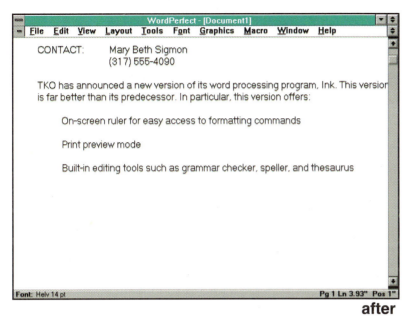
**after**

You see a message that says the spelling check is complete and asks whether you want to close the speller.

6. Click on **OK**.

   This step clears the message. The Speller box remains open.

**Use other options**
WordPerfect offers many spell-check features, such as finding double words (*the the*). Also, you can add words to the dictionary. For complete information, see *Using WordPerfect 5.2 for Windows,* Special Edition.

## REVIEW

1. Click on **Tools** in the menu bar.
2. Click on the **Speller** command.
3. Click on the **Start** button.
4. When WordPerfect stops on a word, do one of the following:
   - Select **Skip Once** to skip this occurrence of the word, but stop on the next one.
   - Select **Skip Always** to skip all occurrences of this word.
   - Select **Add** to add the word to the dictionary.
   - Select **Replace** to replace the word.
5. When the spelling check is complete, click **Yes** to close the speller.

# To check spelling

**Try a shortcut**
Press the Ctrl+F1 key combination to select the Speller command.

**Advanced Editing and Formatting**

123

# TASK

## Use the thesaurus

**Oops!**
To undo the replacement, select Undo from the Edit menu immediately after making the replacement.

before

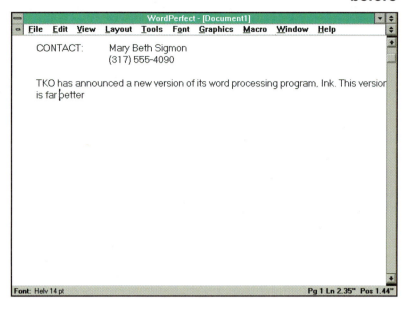

1. Click before the word *better*.

   *Better* is the word that you want to look up in the thesaurus. You can click either before or within the word that you are looking up.

2. Click on **Tools** in the menu bar.

   This step opens the Tools menu. You see a list of Tools commands.

3. Click on **Thesaurus**.

   This step selects the Thesaurus command. The Thesaurus dialog box appears on-screen with a list of synonyms for the selected word.

   The thesaurus has its own menu system.

4. Click on **superior**.

   This step selects the word *superior*. The selected word appears in the Word text box at the bottom of the dialog box. (Notice that the document window might be scrolled, as in the After screen.)

5. Click on Replace.

   The original word (*better*) is replaced with the new word (*superior*).

*Easy* WordPerfect for Windows

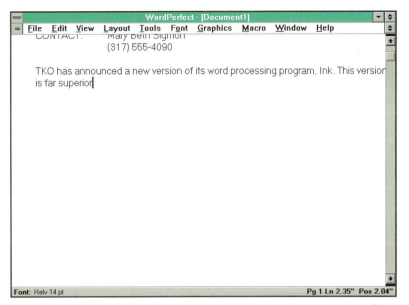
after

**Other options**
The Thesaurus feature offers many choices, such as displaying additional synonyms. For more information, see *Using WordPerfect 5.2 for Windows,* Special Edition.

# REVIEW

## To use the thesaurus

1. Select the word you want to look up.
2. Click on **Tools** in the menu bar.
3. Click on the **Thesaurus** command.
4. If you want to replace the original word, click on the word you want; then click on **Replace**.

**Try a shortcut**
Press the Alt+F1 key combination to select the Thesaurus command.

# TASK

## Count words

before

**Oops!**
To close the Word Count dialog box, click on OK.

1. Click on **Tools** in the menu bar.

   This step opens the Tools menu. You see a list of Tools commands.

2. Click on **Word Count**.

   This step selects the Word Count command. WordPerfect counts the number of words in your document and displays the Word Count dialog box with the results.

   If you are a student or a professional writer, your teacher or editor may want to know the word count.

3. Click on **OK**.

   This step closes the Word Count dialog box.

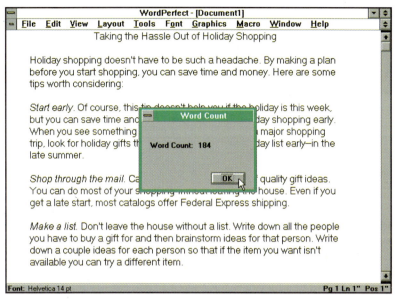

**after**

**Count selected text**
To count just the words in a section of a document, select the text; then select the Word Count command.

## REVIEW

1. Click on **Tools** in the menu bar.
2. Click on the **Word Count** command.
3. Click on the **OK** button.

## To count words

Advanced Editing and Formatting

# TASK

## Alphabetize text

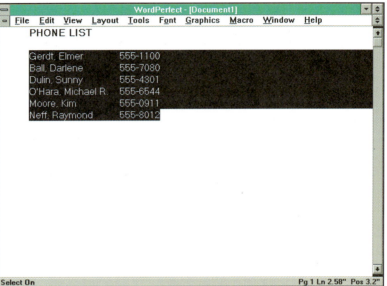

before

**Oops!**
To undo the sort, select Undo from the Edit menu.

1. Select the list of names and phone numbers.

   You can use either the mouse or the keyboard to select text. To use the mouse, hold down the mouse button, drag across the text you want to select, and then release the mouse button. To use the keyboard, hold down the Shift key and use the arrow keys to select the text. See *TASK: Select text* for more information.

   Be sure to select just the list of names and numbers—don't select the heading (PHONE LIST).

2. Click on **Tools** in the menu bar.

   This step opens the Tools menu. You see a list of Tools commands.

3. Click on **Sort**.

   This step selects the Sort command. You see the Sort dialog box. The options in this box control how a sort is performed (the record type, sort order, key definition, and record selection).

   For this task, the default settings are acceptable—that is, you want to sort the lines in ascending order by the first word in the first column (field).

4. Click on **OK**.

   This step selects the OK button. The selected text is sorted alphabetically. While the sort is in progress, you see the Sort Status alert box.

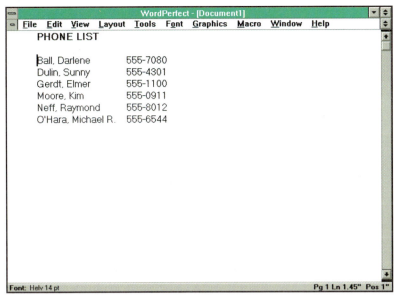

**after**

---

## REVIEW

# To alphabetize text

1. Select the text you want to sort.
2. Click on **Tools** in the menu bar.
3. Click on the **Sort** command.
4. If necessary, change any of the sort options.
5. Click on the **OK** button.

**Try a shortcut**
Press the Ctrl+Shift+F12 key combination to select the Sort command.

**Use other options**
You can sort on more than one key (item), and you can sort different types of text (lines, paragraphs, and so on). See *Using WordPerfect 5.2 for Windows,* Special Edition, for complete information.

# TASK

## Change the case of text

before

**Oops!**
To reverse the change, follow this same procedure to change the text back. The Edit Undo command will not reverse this change.

1. Select the word *free*.
   You can use either the mouse or the keyboard to select text. To use the mouse, hold down the mouse button, drag across the text you want to select, and then release the mouse button. To use the keyboard, hold down the Shift key and use the arrow keys to select the text. See TASK: *Select text* for more information.

2. Click on **Edit** in the menu bar.
   This step opens the Edit menu. You see a list of Edit commands.

3. Click on **Convert Case**.
   This step selects the Convert Case command. You see another list of options.

4. Click on **Uppercase**.
   This step selects the Uppercase command; the text is converted from lowercase to uppercase.

5. Press →.
   This step deselects the text. You also can deselect text by clicking outside the text.

after

# REVIEW

## To change the case of text

1. Select the text you want to change.

2. Click on **Edit** in the menu bar.

3. Click on the **Convert Case** command.

4. Click on the option you want: **Uppercase** or **Lowercase**.

5. Deselect text by pressing any arrow key or clicking outside the selected text.

# TASK

## Display the Ruler

**Oops!**
Follow this same procedure to hide the Ruler.

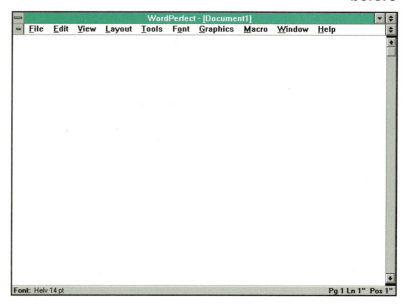

before

1. Click on **View** in the menu bar.

   This step opens the View menu. You see a list of View commands.

2. Click on **Ruler**.

   This step selects the Ruler command and displays the Ruler on-screen.

   You can make formatting changes quickly with the Ruler displayed on-screen. You can change tabs, fonts, font sizes, left and right margins, line spacing, and other formatting options. See *Using WordPerfect 5.2 for Windows,* Special Edition, for complete information on the Ruler.

   The Ruler command is a toggle. Select the command again to hide the Ruler.

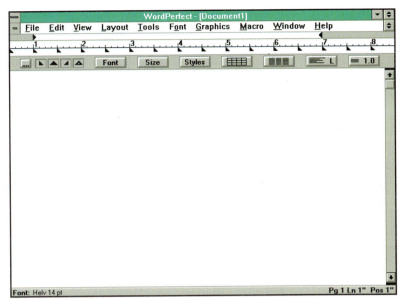
after

**Try a shortcut**
Press the Alt+Shift+F3 key combination to display/hide the Ruler.

1. Click on **View** in the menu bar.
2. Click on the **Ruler** command.

**REVIEW**

**To display the Ruler**

Advanced Editing and Formatting

133

# TASK

## Display the Button Bar

before

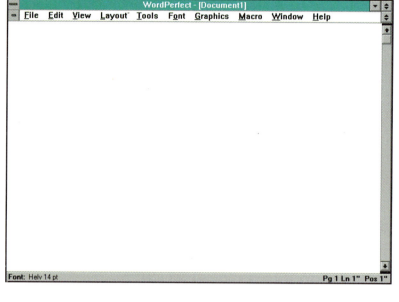

**Oops!**
Follow this same procedure to hide the Button Bar.

1. Click on **View** in the menu bar.

   This step opens the View menu. You see a list of View commands.

2. Click on **Button Bar**.

   This step selects the Button Bar command and displays the default Button Bar on-screen. You can access commands (Save, Print, and others) quickly from the Button Bar. You also can customize your Button Bar. See *Using WordPerfect 5.2 for Windows,* Special Edition, for complete information.

   The Button Bar command is a toggle. Select the command again to hide the Button Bar.

   The View menu indicates whether the Button Bar is displayed or hidden. When the Button Bar is displayed, a check mark appears next to the Button Bar command on the View menu.

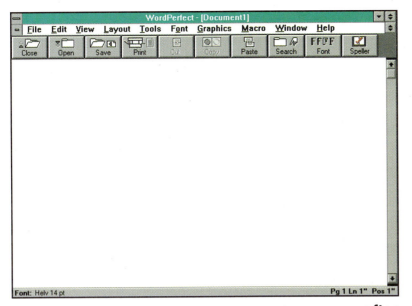

**after**

1. Click on **View** in the menu bar.
2. Click on the **Button Bar** command.

### REVIEW

## To display the Button Bar

**Advanced Editing and Formatting**

## TASK

## Set tabs

**Oops!**
Click on Cancel for step 9 to cancel the changes.

before

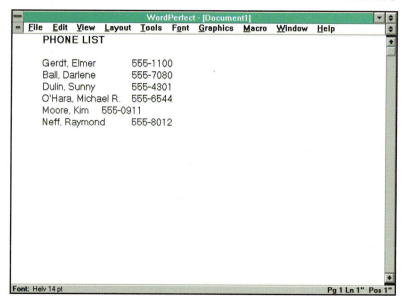

1. Press **Ctrl+Home**.

   Pressing the Ctrl+Home key combination moves the insertion point to the top of the document to ensure that the tab changes affect the entire document.

2. Click on **Layout** in the menu bar.

   This step opens the Layout menu. You see a list of Layout commands.

3. Click on **Line**.

   This step selects the Line command and displays a menu of Line options.

4. Click on **Tab Set**.

   This step selects the Tab Set command. You see the Tab Set dialog box. This box enables you to control the position and type of tabs in the document.

5. Click on **Clear Tabs**.

   This step selects the Clear Tabs button. All the tabs are cleared so that you can set new tabs.

6. Click in the **Relative Position** text box.

   This step moves the insertion point to the Relative Position text box so that you can set the tab.

7. Type **3**.

   This step sets the location for the tab at three inches from the left margin.

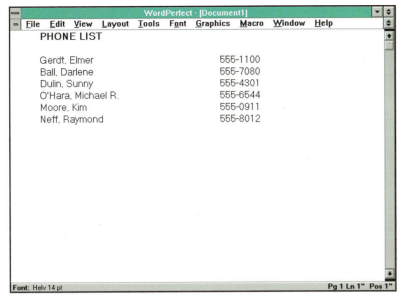

**after**

**Delete tab settings**
To revert to the default tab settings, display Reveal Codes (press the Alt+F3 key combination or select Reveal Codes from the View menu). Then delete the [Tab Set] code.

8. Click on **Set Tab**.
   This step selects the Set Tab button.

9. Click on **OK**.
   This step confirms the new tab setting and closes the dialog box.

# REVIEW

# To set tabs

1. Press **Ctrl+Home** to move to the top of the document.
2. Click on **Layout** in the menu bar.
3. Click on the **Line** command.
4. Click on the **Tab Set** command.
5. If you want, click on the **Clear Tabs** button to clear the tab settings.
6. Click in the **Relative Position** box and type the location of the tab you want to add.
7. Click on the **Tab Set** button.
8. Continue typing the tab position and clicking **Tab Set** for each tab you want to set.
9. Click on the **OK** button to confirm the tab settings.

**Use other tab types**
You can choose different types of tab stops—right, decimal, center. You also can insert a dot leader before a tab stop. See *Using WordPerfect 5.2 for Windows,* Special Edition, for more information on tabs.

# TASK

## Double-space a document

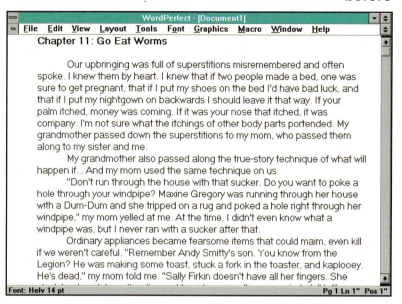

**before**

**Oops!**
Click on Cancel for step 6 to close the dialog box without changing the line spacing of your document.

1. Press **Ctrl+Home**.

   This step moves the insertion point to the top of the document to ensure that the spacing change affects the entire document.

2. Click on **Layout** in the menu bar.

   This step opens the Layout menu. You see a list of Layout commands.

3. Click on **Line**.

   This step selects the Line command and displays a menu of Line options.

4. Click on **Spacing**.

   This step selects the Spacing command. You see the Spacing dialog box. The insertion point is positioned in the Spacing text box; next to this box are an up arrow and a down arrow.

5. Type **2**.

   This step tells WordPerfect to double-space your document.

6. Click on **OK**.

   This step confirms the new spacing interval. The text is double-spaced.

*Easy* **WordPerfect for Windows**

after

**Revert to single spacing**
To revert to single spacing, display Reveal Codes (press the Alt+F3 key combination or select Reveal Codes from the View menu). Then delete the [Ln Spacing:2] code.

## REVIEW

## To double-space a document

1. Press **Ctrl+Home** to position the insertion point at the top of the document.
2. Click on **Layout** in the menu bar.
3. Click on the **Line** command.
4. Click on the **Spacing** command.
5. Type **2** to double-space the document or click on the arrows to display other spacing intervals.
6. Click on the **OK** button.

**Use a different method**
You also can click the up and down arrows next to the spacing box to select a spacing interval for step 5. Values start at .5 and increase by half-inch intervals.

Advanced Editing and Formatting

# TASK

## Set margins

**Oops!**
To cancel the change, click Cancel for step 8 in the Task section.

before

1. Press **Ctrl+Home**.
   Pressing the Ctrl+Home key combination moves the insertion point to the top of the document to ensure that the margin change affects the entire document.

2. Click on **Layout** in the menu bar.
   This step opens the Layout menu. You see a list of Layout commands.

3. Click on **Margins**.
   This step selects the Margins command and displays the Margins dialog box. You see text boxes for each of the four margins: Left, Right, Top, and Bottom. The insertion point is positioned in the Left text box.

4. Type **2** in the Left text box.
   This step specifies a 2-inch left margin.

5. Press **Tab** and type **2**.
   This step specifies a 2-inch right margin.

6. Press **Tab** and type **2**.
   This step specifies a 2-inch top margin.

7. Press **Tab** and type **2**.
   This step specifies a 2-inch bottom margin.

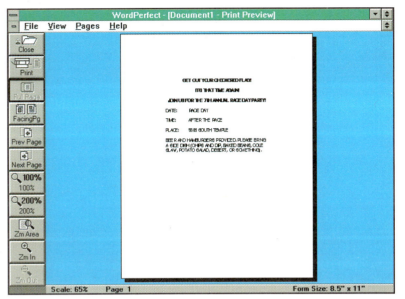

**after**

8. Click on **OK**.

   This step confirms the new margin settings, closes the dialog box, and returns you to the document. You see the effect of the left and right margin changes on-screen. To see the effect of the top and bottom margin changes, you must preview your document. (See *TASK: Preview a document*.) The After screen shows a full-page document preview.

**Restore the default margins**
To return to the default margins, turn on Reveal Codes (press the Alt+F3 key combination or select Reveal Codes from the View menu). Then delete the [L/R Mar:2"2"] and [T/B Mar:2"2"] code.

# REVIEW

## To set margins

1. Press **Ctrl+Home** to place the insertion point at the beginning of the document.
2. Click on **Layout** in the menu bar.
3. Click on the **Margins** command.
4. Type the new margin setting in the appropriate text box (**Left**, **Right**, **Top**, or **Bottom**).
5. Click on the **OK** button.

**Try a shortcut**
Press the Ctrl+F8 key combination to select the Margins command.

# TASK

## Number pages

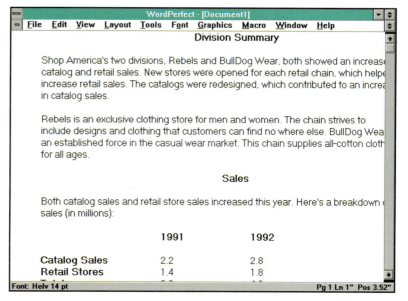
before

**Oops!**
If you change your mind, click on Cancel for step 7 of the Task section.

1. Press **Ctrl**+**Home**.

   This step moves the insertion point to the top of the document to ensure that all pages will be numbered.

2. Click on **Layout** in the menu bar.

   This step opens the Layout menu. You see a list of Layout commands.

3. Click on **Page**.

   This step selects the Page command and displays a menu of Page options. You can also press the Alt+F9 key combination to select this command.

4. Click on **Numbering**.

   This step selects the Numbering command. The Page Numbering dialog box appears. You can use this box to specify many options—position, numbering options, and so on.

5. Click on **Position** and continue holding down the mouse button.

   This step displays a list of position options. (The Position box is in the Define Page Numbering area of the dialog box.) You must hold down the mouse button to display the list of choices.

6. Drag the mouse down to highlight **Bottom Center**.

   This step tells WordPerfect to insert page numbers at the bottom center of every page. You see a sample of the numbering placement under Sample Facing Pages in the dialog box.

*Easy* WordPerfect for Windows

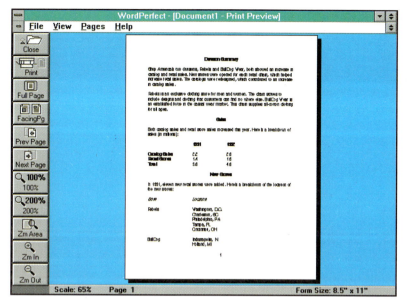

**after**

7. Click on **OK**.

   This step confirms the page numbering setting, closes the dialog box, and returns you to the document. You cannot see the page numbers on-screen. To do so, you must preview your document. (See *TASK: Preview a document*.) The After screen shows a full-page preview of the document.

**Turn off page numbering**
To turn off page numbering, turn on Reveal Codes (press the Alt+F3 key combination or select Reveal Codes from the View menu). Then delete the `[Pg Numbering]` code.

## REVIEW

## To number pages

1. Press **Ctrl+Home** to place the insertion point at the top of the document.
2. Click on **Layout** in the menu bar.
3. Click on the **Page** command.
4. Click on the **Numbering** command.
5. Select the page numbering position that you want.
6. Click on the **OK** button.

**Use other options**
For complete information on all page numbering options, see *Using WordPerfect 5.2 for Windows,* Special Edition.

Advanced Editing and Formatting

# TASK

## Create a header

**before**

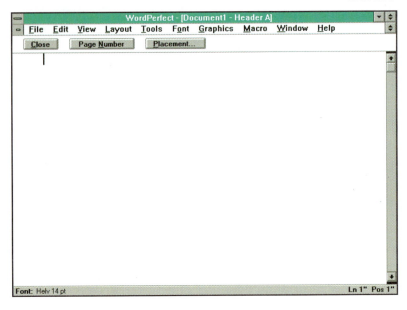

**Oops!**
To close the dialog box without creating a header, click on Cancel for step 4. (If you change your mind when you get to the editing screen, you can no longer cancel. You must delete the header code.)

1. Press **Ctrl**+**Home**.
   This step moves your insertion point to the top of the document to ensure that the new header will be inserted on every page of the document.

2. Click on **Layout** in the menu bar.
   This step opens the Layout menu. You see a list of Layout commands.

3. Click on **Page**.
   This step selects the Page command and displays a menu of Page options.

4. Click on **Headers**.
   This step selects the Headers command. You see the Headers dialog box. Header A is selected.

   You can create a second header by selecting Header B in the dialog box. You might, for example, create one header for odd pages and a second header for even pages.

5. Click on **Create**.
   This step selects the Create button. You see the Header window. (The Before screen shows this step; Header A appears in the title bar.)

6. Type **Annual Report**.
   This is the text you want to print at the top of every page.

*Easy* **WordPerfect for Windows**

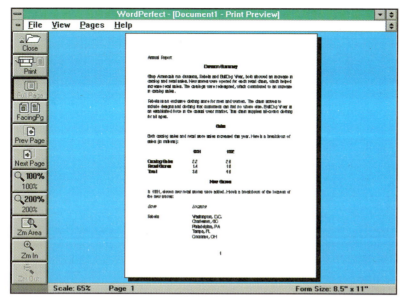

**after**

7. Click on **Close**.

    This step confirms the header and closes the Header window. The header code is inserted into your document, but you don't see the header text on the document screen.

    To see the header, you must preview your document. (See *TASK: Preview a document*.) The After screen shows a full-page preview of the document.

**Delete the header**
To delete the header, turn on Reveal Codes (press the Alt+F3 key combination or select Reveal Codes from the View menu). Then delete the [Header] code.

# REVIEW

# To create a header

1. Press the **Ctrl**+**Home** key combination.
2. Click on **Layout** in the menu bar.
3. Click on the **Page** command.
4. Click on the **Headers** command.
5. Click on the **Create** button.
6. Type the text for the header.
7. Click on the **Close** button.

**Include page numbers**
To include page numbers in the header, select Page Number in the Header window.

**Advanced Editing and Formatting**

# TASK

## Edit a header

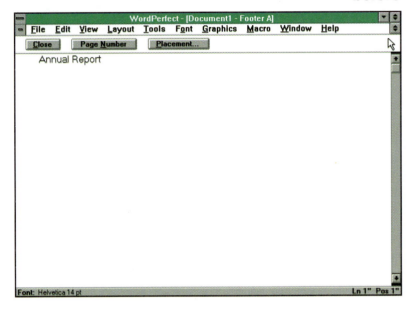

before

**Oops!**
To delete the header, turn on Reveal Codes (press the Alt+F3 key combination or select Reveal Codes from the View menu). Then delete the [Header] code.

1. Click on **Layout** in the menu bar.

   This step opens the Layout menu. You see a list of Layout commands.

2. Click on **Page**.

   This step selects the Page command and displays a menu of Page options.

3. Click on **Headers**.

   This step selects the Headers command. You see the Headers dialog box. The default header (A) is selected; this is the header you want to edit.

4. Click on **Edit**.

   This step selects the Edit button. WordPerfect finds Header A, opens the Header window, and displays the current header text. The Before screen shows this step.

5. Type **1992**.

   *1992* is the additional text you want to print at the top of every page.

6. Press the **space bar**.

   This step inserts a space between the new text and the original text. The complete entry should read *1992 Annual Report*. The After figure shows this step.

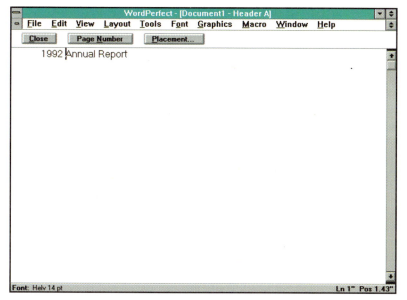

**after**

7. Click on **Close**.

   This step confirms the header and closes the Header window. The header code is inserted into your document, but you don't see the header text on the document screen.

   To see the header, you must preview your document. (See *TASK: Preview a document*.)

**Include page numbers**
To include page numbers in the header, select Page Numbers in the Header window.

# REVIEW

# To edit a header

1. Click on **Layout** in the menu bar.
2. Click on the **Page** command.
3. Click on the **Headers** command.
4. Select the header you want to edit.
5. Click on the **Edit** button.
6. Make any editing changes.
7. Click on the **Close** button.

**Format text**
You can select and format the text in a header—change the font, change the alignment, and so on—as you would format any other text in a document.

# TASK

## Create a footer

before

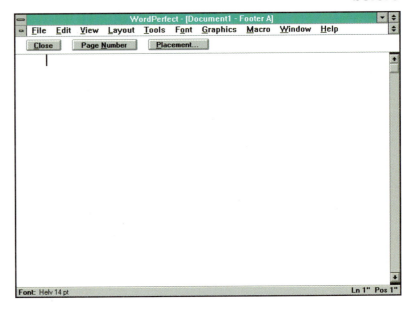

**Oops!**
To close the dialog box without creating a footer, click on Cancel for step 4 of the Task section.

1. Press **Ctrl+Home**.

   This step places the insertion point at the top of the document to ensure that the footer is inserted on every page of the document.

2. Click on **Layout** in the menu bar.

   This step opens the Layout menu. You see a list of Layout commands.

3. Click on **Page**.

   This step selects the Page command and displays a menu of Page options.

4. Click on **Footers**.

   This step selects the Footers command. You see the Footers dialog box. Footer A is selected.

   You can create a second footer by selecting Footer B in the Select area of the dialog box. You might, for example, create one footer for odd pages and a second footer for even pages.

5. Click on **Create**.

   This step selects the Create button. You see the Footer window. `Footer A` appears in the title bar. The Before screen shows this step.

6. Type **Chapter 11**.

   This is the text that you want to print at the bottom of every page.

148

*Easy* **WordPerfect for Windows**

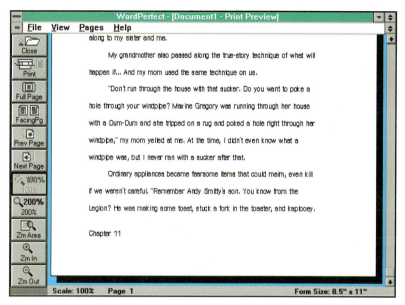

**after**

**Delete the footer**
To delete the footer, turn on Reveal Codes (press the Alt+F3 key combination or select Reveal Codes from the View menu). Then delete the [Footer] code.

7. Click on **Close**.

   This step confirms the header and closes the Footer window. The Footer code is inserted into your document, but you don't see the footer text on the document screen.

   To see the footer, you must preview your document. (See *TASK: Preview a document*.) The After screen shows a 100% preview of the bottom of the document.

# REVIEW

## To create a footer

1. Press the **Ctrl+Home** key combination.
2. Click on **Layout** in the menu bar.
3. Click on the **Page** command.
4. Click on the **Footers** command.
5. Click on the **Create** button.
6. Type the text for the footer.
7. Click on the **Close** button.

**Include page numbers**
To include page numbers in the footer, select Page Numbers in the Footer window.

**Advanced Editing and Formatting**

**149**

## TASK

## Edit a footer

before

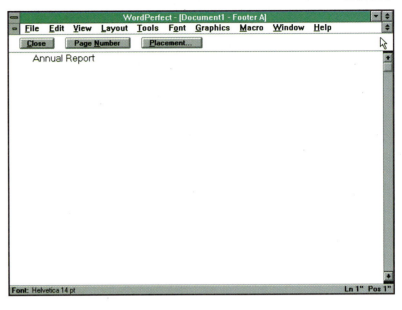

**Oops!**
To delete the footer, turn on Reveal Codes (press the Alt+F3 key combination or select Reveal Codes from the View menu). Then delete the [Footer] code.

1. Click on **Layout** in the menu bar.

   This step opens the Layout menu. You see a list of Layout commands.

2. Click on **Page**.

   This step selects the Page command and displays a menu of Page options.

3. Click on **Footers**.

   This step selects the Footers command. You see the Footers dialog box. The default footer (A) is selected; this is the footer you want to edit.

4. Click on **Edit**.

   This step selects the Edit button. You see the Footer window with the current footer text. The Before screen shows this step.

5. Press **End**.

   Pressing the End key moves the insertion point to the end of the line.

6. Press **Alt**+**F7**.

   Pressing the Alt+F7 key combination selects the Flush Right command. The insertion point moves to the right margin.

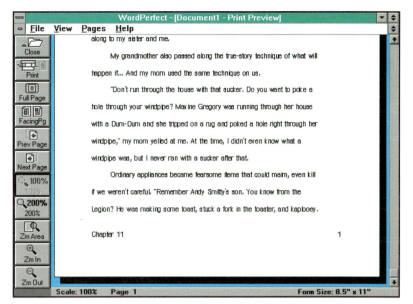

**after**

**Format text**
You can select and format the text in a footer—change the font, change the alignment, and so on—as you would any other text in the document.

7. Click on **Page Number**.

   This step inserts the page number at the right margin. The code ^B indicates the page number.

8. Click on **Close**.

   This step confirms the footer and closes the Footer window. The footer code is inserted into your document, but you don't see the footer text on the document screen.

   To see the footer, you must preview your document. (See *TASK: Preview a document*.) The After screen shows a 100% view of the bottom of the document.

## REVIEW

## To edit a footer

1. Click on **Layout** in the menu bar.
2. Click on the **Page** command.
3. Click on the **Footers** command.
4. Select the footer you want to edit.
5. Click on the **Edit** button.
6. Make any editing changes.
7. Click on the **Close** command.

**Advanced Editing and Formatting**

**151**

# TASK

## Center a page

**before**

**Oops!**
To undo the change, immediately select the Undo command from the Edit menu. Or display Reveal Codes (press the Alt+F3 key combination) and delete the [Center Pg] code.

1. Click on **Layout** in the menu bar.

   This step opens the Layout menu and displays a list of Layout commands.

2. Click on **Page**.

   This step selects the Page command and displays a list of Page commands.

3. Click on **Center Page**.

   This step inserts a code into your document. You cannot see the change on-screen. To see the change, preview your document. See *TASK: Preview a document*. The After screen shows a full-page preview.

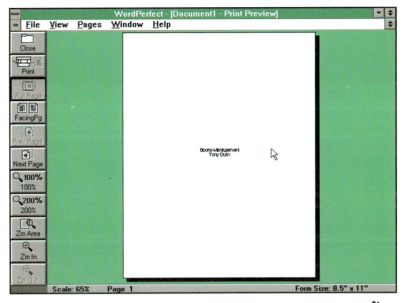

after

# REVIEW

1. Click on **Layout** in the menu bar.
2. Click on the **Page** command.
3. Click on the **Center Page** command.

## To center a page

# TASK

## Draw a horizontal line

**Oops!**
To delete the line, select Undo from the Edit menu immediately after inserting the line.

**before**

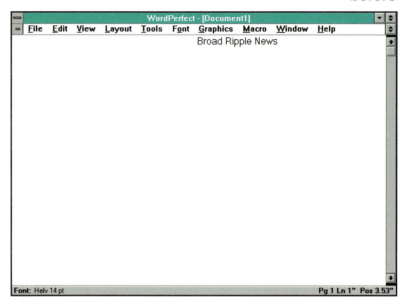

1. Click after *Broad Ripple News* and press **Enter**.
   This step ends the first line and begins a new line. This new line is where you want to insert the horizontal line.

2. Click on **Graphics** in the menu bar.
   This step opens the Graphics menu. You see a list of Graphics commands.

3. Click on **Line**.
   This step selects the Line command. You see a list of Line options.

4. Click on **Horizontal**.
   This step displays the Horizontal Line dialog box. With the settings in this box, you can control line size, vertical position, horizontal position, and gray shading. For this task, you will use the default settings.

5. Click on **OK**.
   This step accepts the default settings—full line (margin to margin), 0.13 inches thick, 100% gray shading. WordPerfect inserts a code that describes your line and displays the line on-screen.

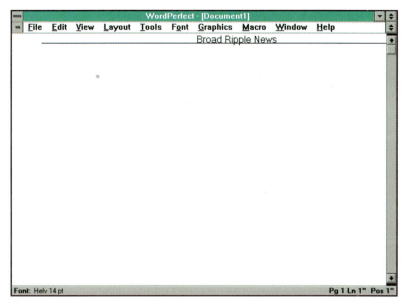

after

**Experiment with lines**
You can change the position, length, width, and shading of the line. You also can create a variety of vertical lines and other graphics. Experiment with the settings in the dialog box. Or see *Using WordPerfect 5.2 for Windows,* Special Edition, for more information on these options.

# REVIEW

## To draw a horizontal line

1. Place the insertion point in the spot where you want to insert the line.
2. Click on **Graphics** in the menu bar.
3. Click on the **Line** command.
4. Click on **Horizontal**.
5. Click on the **OK** button to accept the default line settings.

**Delete a line**
To delete a line, turn on Reveal Codes (press the Alt+F3 key combination or select Reveal Codes from the View menu). Then delete the [HLine] code.

Advanced Editing and Formatting

# TASK

## Insert a special character

**before**

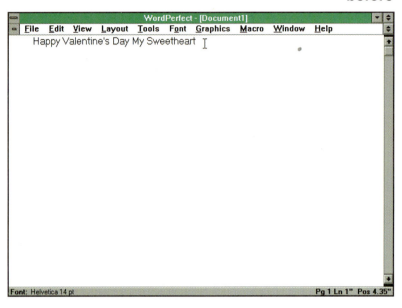

**Oops!**
If you don't want to insert the character, select Close for step 4 of the Task section.

1. Click on **Font** in the menu bar.
   This step opens the Font menu and displays Font commands.

2. Click on **WP Characters**.
   This step selects the WP Characters command. You see the WordPerfect Characters dialog box. This box lists the selected set, displays the characters within that set, and lists the number of the selected character.

3. Click on the down arrow next to Set and hold down the mouse button. Drag down until you select **Iconic Symbols**; then release the mouse button.
   This step selects the Iconic Symbols set. You see the characters in this set. The first character, a heart, is selected.

4. Click on **Insert and Close**.
   This step inserts the symbol and closes the dialog box.

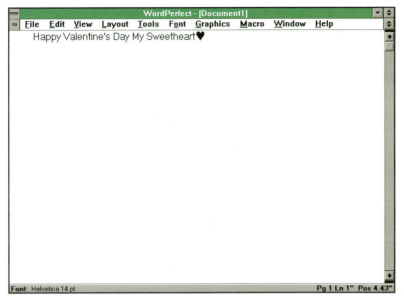

**after**

1. Click on **Font** in the menu bar.
2. Click on the **WP Characters** command.
3. Select the character set that you want.
4. Click on the character that you want to insert.
5. Click on the **Insert and Close** button.

## REVIEW

**Delete the character**
Delete the special character as you would any other character: press the Delete or Backspace key.

# To insert a special character

**Try a shortcut**
Press the Ctrl+W key combination to select the WP Characters command.

Advanced Editing and Formatting

# TASK

## Insert a graphic

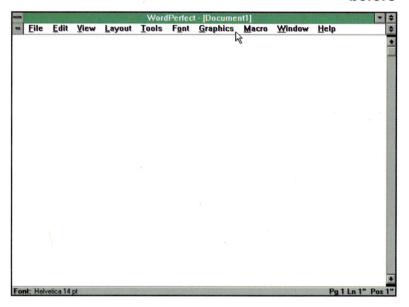
before

**Oops!**
To undo the insertion, immediately select the Undo command from the Edit menu. Or press the Alt+F3 key combination to display the Reveal Codes and delete the [Fig Box] code. Or click on the graphic, which causes a dotted box to surround the graphic; press the Del key.

1. Click on **Graphics** in the menu bar.
   This step opens the Graphics menu and displays a list of Graphics commands.

2. Click on **Figure**.
   This step selects the type of box that you want to insert—a figure box. You also can select other box types. A submenu appears.

3. Click on **Retrieve**.
   This step selects the Retrieve command. You see the Retrieve Figure dialog box, which includes files and directories lists. WordPerfect includes several graphics (wpg files).

4. In the Files list, click on **birthday.wpg**.
   This step selects the graphic that you want to insert.

5. Click on **Retrieve**.
   The graphic is inserted on-screen in the default position and size. You can change the box position and size. (For information, see *Using WordPerfect 5.2 for Windows,* Special Edition.)

after

## REVIEW

### To insert a graphic

1. Click on **Graphics** in the menu bar.
2. Click on the **Figure** command.
3. Click on the **Retrieve** command.
4. In the Files list, click on the graphic that you want.
5. Click on the **Retrieve** button.

**Can't see the graphic?**
If you cannot see the graphic on-screen, check the View menu. Be sure that a check mark appears next to the Graphics option. If there is no check mark next to Graphics, click on that command.

**Use other options**
WordPerfect offers many types of graphics and graphics boxes. You also can move and resize the graphics. For complete information, see *Using WordPerfect 5.2 for Windows,* Special Edition.

# TASK

## Move a graphic

before

**Oops!**
Follow this same procedure to move the graphic back to its original location.

1. Click on the graphic.
   This step selects the graphic that you want to move. A dotted rectangle surrounds the graphic, and a four-headed arrow appears when the mouse pointer is positioned on the graphic.

2. Click and hold down the mouse button and drag the graphic to the upper left corner of the screen.
   This step moves the graphic to the new location.

3. Release the mouse button.
   The graphic is placed and still selected.

4. Click outside the graphic.
   This step deselects the graphic.

**after**

1. Click on the graphic.
2. Click and hold down the mouse and drag the graphic to the new location.
3. Release the mouse button.
4. Click outside the graphic.

**Try other options**
For information on other box position and size options, see *Using WordPerfect 5.2 for Windows,* Special Edition.

### REVIEW

## To move a graphic

Advanced Editing and Formatting

161

# TASK

## Insert a table

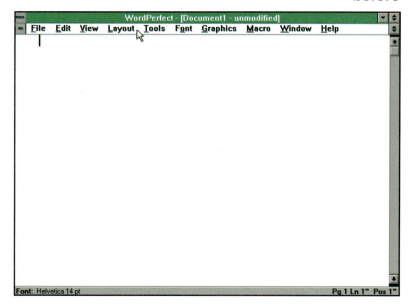

before

**Oops!**
To undo the table, immediately select the Undo command from the Edit menu. Or press the Alt+F3 key combination to display Reveal Codes; then delete the [Tbl Def] code.

1. Click on **Layout** in the menu bar.
   This step opens the Layout menu and displays a list of Layout commands.

2. Click on **Tables**.
   This step selects the Tables command.

3. Click on **Create**.
   This step selects the Create command. You see the Create Table dialog box. This dialog box enables you to specify the number of columns and rows in the table. By default the table has three columns.

4. Press **Tab**.
   Pressing the Tab key accepts the default number of columns and moves to the Rows text box.

5. Type **3**.
   This step tells WordPerfect to create a table with three rows.

6. Click on **OK**.
   This step confirms the table definition and inserts a table with three columns and three rows on-screen.

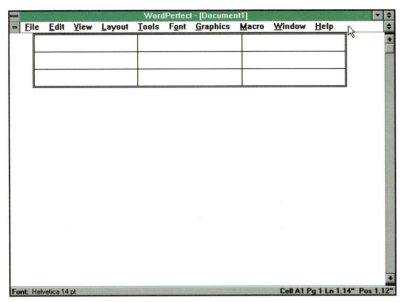

**after**

**Need more information?**
For more information on the Tables command, see *Using WordPerfect 5.2 for Windows,* Special Edition.

# REVIEW

## To insert a table

1. Click on **Layout** in the menu bar.
2. Click on the **Tables** command.
3. Click on the **Create** command.
4. Type the number of columns you want and press **Tab**.
5. Type the number of rows you want.
6. Click on the **OK** button.

# TASK

## Enter text into a table

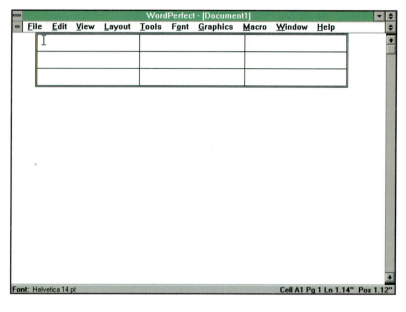

**before**

**Oops!**
To edit text in a cell, use any of the editing techniques and keystrokes you would use in a regular document.

1. Type **Project** and press **Tab**.
   This step enters information into the first cell in the table and moves the insertion point to the next column in that row. A *cell* is the intersection of a row and column.

2. Type **Team Leader** and press **Tab**.
   This step enters information in that cell and moves the insertion point to the next column.

3. Type **Goal** and press **Tab**.
   This step completes the headings for the tables. Follow steps 4 through 9 to enter information in the other cells.

4. Type **Crime Watch** and press **Tab**.

5. Type **Michael O'Hara** and press **Tab**.

6. Type **Set up a neighborhood Crime Watch program** and press **Tab**.

7. Type **Recycle** and press **Tab**.

8. Type **Alana Moore** and press **Tab**.

9. Type **Involve more neighbors in the recycling program**.
   This step completes the text for the table.

*Easy* **WordPerfect for Windows**

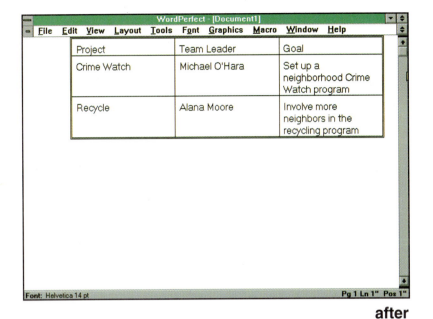

**after**

1. Type the text in the first cell and press **Tab**.

2. Continue typing text and pressing **Tab** until you complete all cells.

**Be careful!**
Don't press Enter in a cell unless you want to insert a line break; press the Tab key instead. Pressing Enter does not move you to the next row.

# R E V I E W

## To enter text into a table

**Want to add rows?**
For more information on adding rows and working with the Table feature, see *Using WordPerfect 5.2 for Windows,* Special Edition.

Advanced Editing and Formatting

165

# Printing

This section includes the following tasks:

Select a printer

Preview a document

Display a document in draft mode

Print the on-screen document

Print selected text

# TASK

## Select a printer

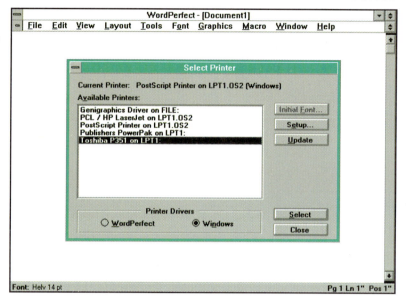

before

**Oops!**
To close the dialog box without selecting a printer, click on Close for step 5.

1. Click on **File** in the menu bar.

   This step opens the File menu. You see a list of File commands.

2. Click on **Select Printer**.

   This step selects the Select Printer command. You see the Select Printer dialog box. (The Before screen shows this step.) This box displays the current printer and lists available printers. The currently selected printer is highlighted.

   From this dialog box you can select the initial font and control other printer settings. For information on all dialog box options, see *Using WordPerfect 5.2 for Windows,* Special Edition.

3. In the Printer Drivers area of the dialog box, click on **Windows**.

   The Printer Drivers area is at the bottom of the dialog box. This step tells WordPerfect to use a Microsoft Windows printer driver (rather than a WordPerfect printer driver).

   If this option is already selected (the circle is darkened), skip this step.

   You see a list of Windows printers. These are printers you have installed through the Windows control panel. (See your Windows documentation or *Using Windows 3.1,* Special Edition, for more information on installing printers.)

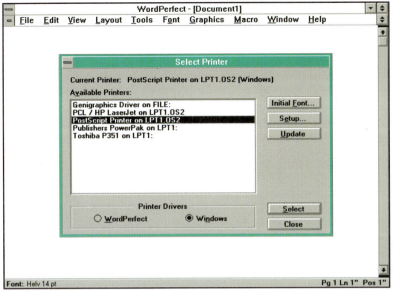

after

4. Click on **PostScript Printer on LPT1.OS2**.

   This step selects the PostScript printer. If you aren't using this printer, find the name of your printer on the list and select it. (The After screen shows this step.)

5. Click on **Select**.

   This step chooses the Select button and tells WordPerfect to use the selected printer to print documents. The dialog box closes, and you return to your document.

   Your printer selection also affects what fonts are available. See *Using WordPerfect 5.2 for Windows,* Special Edition, for complete information on fonts.

### REVIEW

### To select a printer

1. Click on **File** in the menu bar.
2. Click on the **Select Printer** command.
3. Click on **Windows** in the Printer Drivers area of the Select Printer dialog box.
4. Find the name of your printer in the list and select it.
5. Click on the **Select** button.

Printing

169

# TASK

## Preview a document

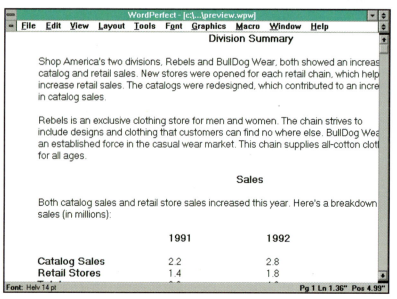
before

**Oops!**
To exit Print Preview, click on the Close button. You also can select Close from the File menu or press the Ctrl+F4 key combination.

1. Click anywhere on the page.

   This step places the insertion point on the page you want to preview.

2. Click on **File** in the menu bar.

   This step opens the File menu and displays a list of File commands.

3. Click on **Print Preview**.

   This step selects the Print Preview command. You see a graphical representation of how your document will look when printed. The buttons along the side of the screen let you change the view.

   The view you see when you select the command is the view you selected last. Print Preview also has its own menu commands.

4. Click on **Full Page**.

   This step selects the Full Pages button, which gives you a full-page view of your document. (The After screen shows this step.) You can see different document elements—headers, footers, page numbers, and so on—that do not appear in normal view.

   You can select different views (100%, 200%), and you can zoom in and out. You also can display full pages and facing pages. See *Using WordPerfect 5.2 for Windows,* Special Edition, for complete information.

5. Click on **Close**.

   This step selects the Close button and closes the Print Preview. You return to your document.

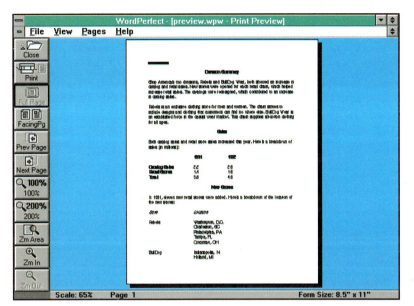
after

**Try a shortcut**
Press the Shift+F5 key combination to select the Print Preview command.

# REVIEW

1. Click on **File** in the menu bar.
2. Click on the **Print Preview** command.
3. If you want to change the view, click on **View** in the menu bar; then click on the view you want. Or click on **Pages**, and select a page option.
4. Click on the **Close** button to exit Print Preview.

# To preview a document

**See other pages**
To view other pages, select the Next Page or Prev Page buttons.

Printing

# TASK

## Display a document in Draft mode

**Oops!**
Draft mode is a toggle; select Draft Mode from the View menu again to turn it off.

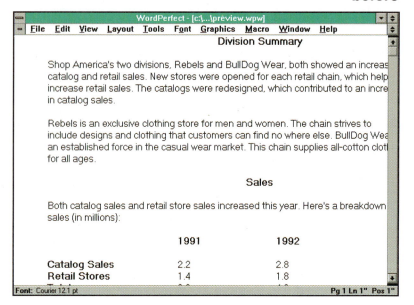

**before**

1. Click on **View** in the menu bar.
   This step opens the View menu. You see a list of View commands.

2. Click on **Draft Mode**.
   This step selects the Draft Mode command. You see your document in draft mode. This mode does not display fonts or font attributes. Instead, text in a different font appears in a different color.

after

**Why use Draft mode?** Draft mode enables you to work much faster within WordPerfect because the program does not have to format on-screen items.

REVIEW

## To display a document in Draft mode

1. Click on **View** in the menu bar.
2. Click on the **Draft Mode** command.

# TASK

## Print the on-screen document

**before**

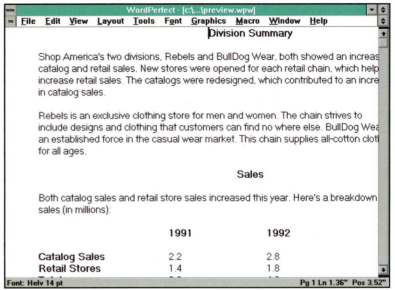

**Oops!**
If you change your mind, click on Close for step 4 to close the dialog box without printing.

1. Click on **File** in the menu bar.
   *This step opens the File menu and displays a list of File commands.*

2. Click on **Print**.
   *This step selects the Print command. You see the Print dialog box. This box lists the current printer. An area for printer options lets you specify what is printed; the Document settings control options such as text and graphics quality. There is also an area in which you can specify the numbers of copies.*

3. Make sure that Full Document is selected in the Options section.
   *The default selection is Full Document. If it isn't selected, click on the Full Document button to select it.*

4. Click on **Print**.
   *This step selects the Print button. The document prints. While the document is printing, you see a status box on-screen. (The After screen shows this step.)*

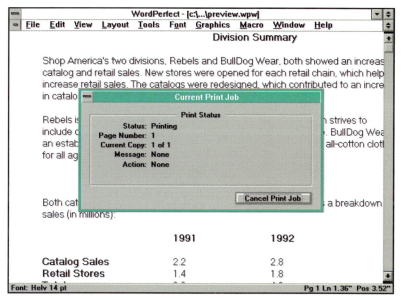

after

**Cancel a print job**
While the document is printing, the Current Print Job dialog box appears on-screen. Click on the Cancel Print Job button to cancel the print job.

## REVIEW

1. Click on **File** in the menu bar.
2. Click on the **Print** command.
3. Select **Full Document** in the Options section.
4. Click on **Print**.

# To print the on-screen document

**Try a shortcut**
Press the F5 key to select the Print command.

# TASK

## Print selected text

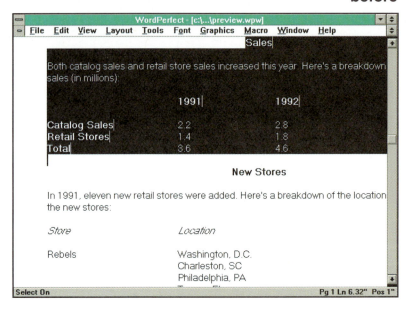

before

**Oops!**
Click on Close for step 4 in the Task section to close the dialog box without printing.

1. Select the Sales section of the report.
   This step selects the text that you want to print. See the Before screen to see which text to select.

2. Click on **File** in the menu bar.
   This step opens the File menu and displays a list of File commands.

3. Click on **Print**.
   This step selects the Print command. You see the Print dialog box. Selected Text is selected in the Options area of the dialog box.

4. Click on **Print**.
   This step selects the Print button. The selected text prints. While the document is printing, you see a status box on-screen. (The After screen shows this step.)

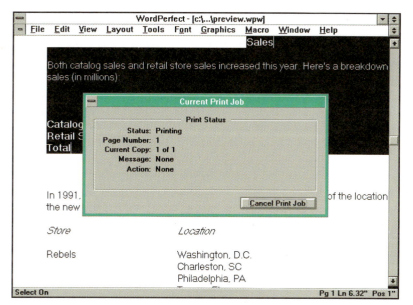

**after**

**Cancel a print job**
While the text is printing, the Current Print Job dialog box appears on-screen. Click on the Cancel Print Job button to cancel the print job.

## REVIEW

1. Select the text you want to print.
2. Click on **File** in the menu bar.
3. Click on the **Print** command.
4. Change any print options, if necessary.
5. Click on the **Print** button.

## To print selected text

**Try a shortcut**
Press the F5 key to select the Print command.

# Merging

This section includes the following tasks:

Create a merge letter

Create a secondary file

Enter a record into the secondary file

Enter other records into the secondary file

Save the secondary file

Create a primary file

Save the primary file

Merge the files

# TASK

## Create a merge letter

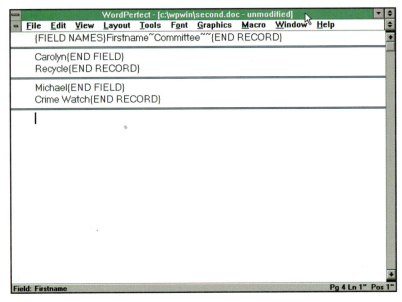

Secondary

**Tasks build on each other**
The tasks in this section all build on each other and follow one right after the other. By the end of this section, you will have created a merge letter.

*Creating a merge letter is an involved process. This task describes the general process and refers you to the specific tasks for help on each step.*

1. Create a secondary file.

   Two files make up a basic merge procedure: the secondary file and the primary file. The primary file contains the unchanging text and the codes that control the merge. The secondary file contains the field definition and the variable information you want inserted into the primary file. You create the secondary file first. See *TASK: Create a secondary file*.

2. Enter the records.

   After you create the secondary file, you enter records. A *record* is one set of information; each record is entered on a separate page. Each individual element in the record is stored in a *field*. You will create a document—with the specific information in that record—for each record you enter. See *TASK: Enter a record into the secondary file* and *TASK: Enter other records into the secondary file*.

3. Save the secondary file.

   After you enter the records, you need to save the secondary file. See *TASK: Save the secondary file*.

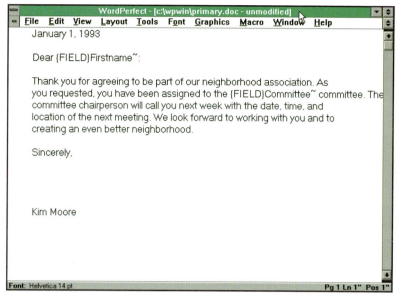
**Primary**

**Need more information?**
WordPerfect's Merge feature offers many options that can make it a complex topic. This book covers only the bare essentials. If you want complete information, see *Using WordPerfect 5.2 for Windows,* Special Edition.

4. **Create a primary file.**

    The primary file contains the text of the letter—the information you want each letter to contain. The primary file also includes the codes that control the merge. You need to know the names of the fields you create in the secondary file so that you can insert the right code into the primary file. For that reason, you create the primary file after you create the secondary file. See *TASK: Create a primary file*.

5. **Save the primary file.**

    After you create the primary file, save the file.

6. **Merge the files.**

    The final step is to merge the two files. A new file will be created that contains a letter for each record in the secondary file. You can save the new file or just print it. See *TASK: Merge the files*.

# TASK

## Create a secondary file
*(Part 1 of 2)*

**before**

**Oops!**
If you don't want to create the file, click on the Cancel button in step 5 of the Task section. The Merge Field Name(s) dialog box will close.

*Creating a secondary file is a two-part process. These two pages contain the first part of this task, Select the field type. Turn the page for the second part, Enter the field names.*

1. Click on **Tools** in the menu bar.

   This step opens the Tools menu. You see a list of Tools commands.

2. Click on **Merge**.

   This step selects the Merge command and displays a submenu.

3. Click on **Merge Codes**.

   This step selects the Merge Codes command and displays the Insert Merge Codes dialog box. This dialog box enables you to insert a code that defines the fields you want to insert into the document.

   A *field* is the variable information in the merge letter—the information that you want to specialize or insert into each letter.

4. Click on **{FIELD NAMES}name1~...nameN~**.

   This is the type of code you want to insert. For information on other merge codes, see *Using WordPerfect 5.2 for Windows, Special Edition*. You may have to scroll through the list to find this code.

*Easy* **WordPerfect for Windows**

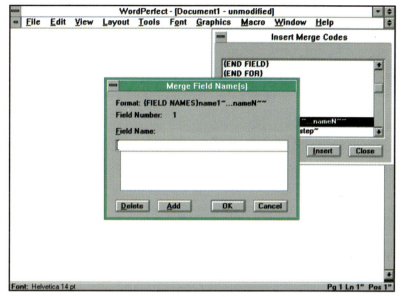

**after**

5. Click on **Insert**.

You see the Merge Field Name(s) dialog box. This dialog box enables you to specify the field number and name.

**What is a secondary file?**
The *secondary merge file* stores the variable information that you want to insert into the primary merge document. Each piece of information is stored in a field; a set of information is called a *record*.

### REVIEW

1. Click on **Tools** in the menu bar.
2. Click on the **Merge** command.
3. Click on the **Merge Codes** command.
4. Click on **{FIELD NAMES}name1~...nameN~**.
5. Click on the **Insert** button.

# To create a secondary file

**Try a shortcut**
Press the Ctrl+F12 key combination to select the Merge command.

Merging

183

# TASK

## Create a secondary file

*(Part 2 of 2)*

**Oops!**
If you don't want to add the fields, click on the Cancel button at any point before step 5 in the Task section. Then click on Close.

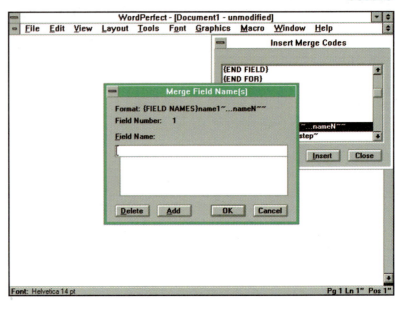

before

*Creating a secondary file is a two-part task. The preceding two pages cover the first part, Select the field type. These two pages contain the second part of the task, Enter the field names.*

1. In the Field Name text box, type **Firstname**.

   This step enters the name for the first field. Be sure that you remember the names of the fields you define. When you create the primary merge file, you will need to type the names exactly as you defined them in this process.

2. Click on **Add**.

   This step adds the first field.

3. Click in the Field Name text box and type **Committee**.

   This step enters the name for the second field. The field number is changed to 2.

4. Click on **Add**.

   This step adds the second field.

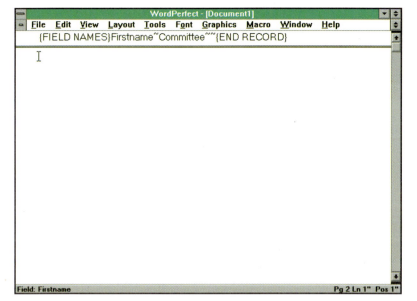

**after**

**Add other fields**
You can add as many fields as you need. And you can add other types of fields. See *Using WordPerfect 5.2 for Windows,* Special Edition, for complete information.

5. Click on **OK**.

   This step closes the Merge Field Name(s) dialog box.

6. Click on **Close**.

   This step closes the Insert Merge Codes dialog box. The first page of the document contains the field definition. A page break is inserted automatically. You start entering specific records on this page.

# REVIEW

## To create a secondary file

1. Type the name of the field in the Field Name text box.
2. Click **Add**.
3. Continue adding fields until you have all you want.
4. Click on the **OK** button.
5. Click on the **Close** button.

Merging

185

# TASK

## Enter a record into the secondary file

**before**

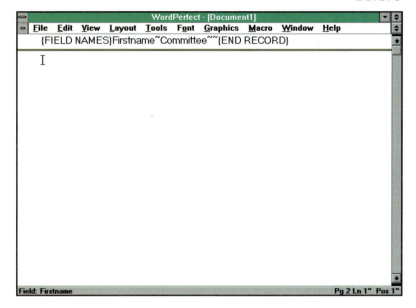

**Oops!**
If you make a mistake when typing, correct it as you would in any other document. All of the editing features are available when you are creating a merge file.

1. Type **Carolyn**.
   This step enters the information for the first field (the Firstname field). When you merge the documents, this specific text will be inserted into the document.

2. Click on **Tools** in the menu bar.
   This step opens the Tools menu.

3. Click on **Merge**.
   This step selects the Merge command.

4. Click on **End Field**.
   This step enters an End Field code and marks, for WordPerfect, the end of the field.

5. Type **Recycle**.
   This step enters the information for the second field.

6. Click on **Tools** in the menu bar.
   This step opens the Tools menu.

7. Click on **Merge**.
   This step selects the Merge command.

8. Click on **End Record**.
   This step enters an End Record code and tells WordPerfect where the record ends. A page break is inserted automatically. Each record is stored on a separate page.

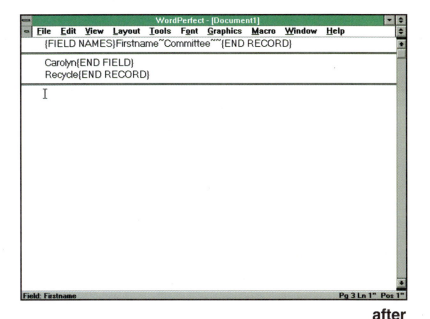

after

**Try a shortcut**
Press the Alt+Enter key combination to enter the End Field code. Press the Alt+Shift+Enter key combination to enter the End Record code.

## REVIEW

## To enter a record into the secondary file

1. Type the information for the field.
2. Click on **Tools** in the menu bar.
3. Click on the **Merge** command.
4. Click on the **End Field** command.
5. Continue typing and marking the end of each field.
6. When all fields have been entered, click on **Tools** in the menu bar.
7. Click on the **Merge** command.
8. Click on the **End Record** command.

**Field vs. record**
A *field* is a piece of information. A *record* is a set of related fields. For example, Last Name, First Name, and Address might be fields in an address database. The record would include the last name, first name, and address for one person.

**Merging**

187

# TASK

## Enter other records into the secondary file

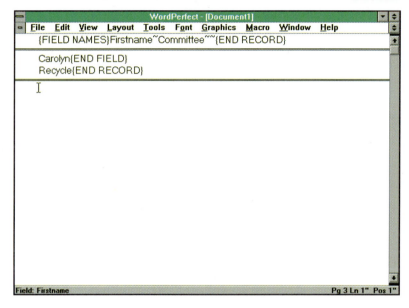

before

**Oops!**
If you make a mistake when typing, correct it as you would in any other document. All of the editing features are available when you are creating a merge file.

1. Type **Michael**.

   This step enters the information in the first field of the second record.

2. Press **Alt**+**Enter**.

   This step enters the End Field code. This key combination is a shortcut. You also can select Tools, Merge, End Field.

3. Type **Crime Watch**.

   This step enters the information for the next field.

4. Press **Shift**+**Alt**+**Enter**.

   This step enters the End Record code. This key combination is a shortcut. You also can select Tools, Merge, End Record.

*Easy* **WordPerfect for Windows**

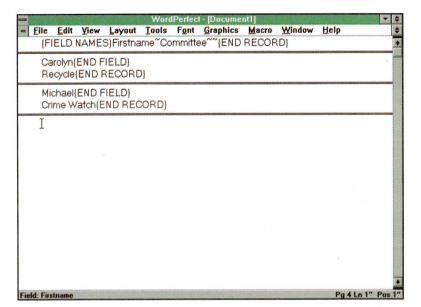

**after**

**Delete a record**
To delete a record, select all the text and codes for that record and press the Delete key.

---

**REVIEW**

1. Type the information for the first field.

2. Press **Alt**+**Enter** or select **Tools**, **Merge**, **End Field**.

3. Continue typing the field information.

4. When you are finished with all the fields, press **Shift**+**Alt**+**Enter** or select **Tools**, **Merge**, **End Record**.

# To enter other records into the secondary file

Merging

189

# TASK

## Save the secondary file

**before**

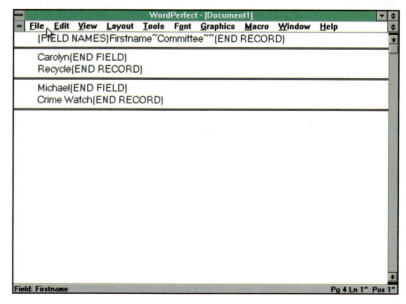

1. Click on **File** in the menu bar.

   This step opens the File menu and displays a list of File commands.

2. Click on **Save**.

   This step selects the Save command. You see the Save As dialog box.

3. Type **SECOND.DOC**.

   This step enters the name for the secondary file.

4. Click on **Save**.

   This step saves the document. The document remains open on-screen and the file name—along with the path—appears in the title bar. For more information on saving, see the tasks in the section "Managing Files."

**Oops!**
If you don't want to save the file, click on the Cancel button for step 4.

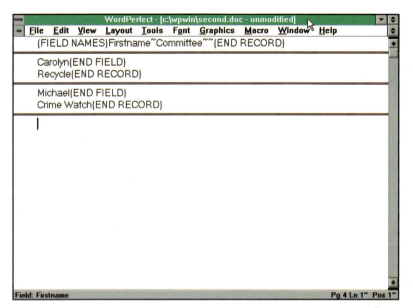

**after**

1. Click on **File** in the menu bar.
2. Click on the **Save** command.
3. Type the file name.
4. Click on the **Save** button.

**Try a shortcut**
Press the Shift+F3 key combination to select the File Save command.

# REVIEW

## To save the secondary file

**Save again**
To save again, select File Save. You won't be prompted for a file name. The file will be saved with the same name.

Merging

191

# TASK

## Create a primary file
*(Part 1 of 2)*

**before**

**Oops!**
Be sure to type the field name correctly. If what you type does not match what you entered when you defined the field in the secondary file, WordPerfect will not alert you to the discrepancy. When you merge the letters, however, nothing will be inserted for that field.

*Creating a primary file is a two-part process. These two pages cover the first part, Insert the first field. Turn the page for the next part, Finish the letter.*

1. Open a new document.
   To open a document, select File, New. See *TASK: Create a new document* for more information.

2. Type **January 1, 1993** and press **Enter twice**. Type **Dear** and press the **space bar**.
   This step enters the beginning text for the primary file. The primary file contains the unchanging text and the merge codes that tell WordPerfect where to insert the changing—or *variable*—information. You are now ready to insert a field.

3. Click on **Tools** in the menu bar.
   This step opens the Tools menu.

4. Click on **Merge**.
   This step selects the Merge command.

5. Click on **Field**.
   This step selects the Field command. You see the Insert Merge Code dialog box. The dialog box contains a text box so that you can enter the field.

**after**

> **Delete a field**
> If you insert the field incorrectly, select it and press the Delete key. Then try again.

6. Type **Firstname** and click **OK**.
   This step inserts the field code into your document. On-screen you see the field code. This code tells WordPerfect to insert the information into the first field of each record.

7. Type **:** and press **Enter twice**.
   This step finishes the greeting for the letter.

# REVIEW

## To create a primary file

1. Open a new document.
2. Type the text you want the letter to include.
3. When you want to insert the first field code, click on **Tools** in the menu bar.
4. Click on the **Merge** command.
5. Click on the **Field** command.
6. Type the field name and click on the **OK** button.

# TASK

## Create a primary file
*(Part 2 of 2)*

**before**

*Creating a primary file is a two-part process. The preceding two pages contain the first part, Insert the first field. These two pages contain the second part of the task, Finish the letter.*

1. Type the middle of the letter:

   **Thank you for agreeing to be part of our neighborhood association. As you requested, you have been assigned to the**

   This step enters more of the unchanging text. Be sure to press the space bar after "the." You are now ready to insert the next field.

2. Click on **Tools** in the menu bar.

   This step opens the Tools menu.

3. Click on **Merge**.

   This step selects the Merge command.

4. Click on **Field**.

   This step selects the Field command. You see the Insert Merge Code dialog box. The dialog box contains a text box so that you can enter the field.

5. Type **committee** and click on **OK**.

   This step inserts the field code into your document. On-screen you will see the field code. This code tells WordPerfect to insert the information into the first field of each record.

**Oops!**
Be sure that you type the field name correctly. If what you type does not match what you entered when you defined the field in the secondary file, WordPerfect will not alert you of the discrepancy. When you merge the letters, however, nothing will be inserted for that field.

**after**

**Delete a field**
If you insert the field incorrectly, select it and press the Delete key. Then try again.

6. Type the rest of the letter:

   **committee. The committee chairperson will call you next week with the date, time, and location of the next meeting. We look forward to working with you and to creating an even better neighborhood.**

   **Sincerely,**

   **Kim Moore**
   This step completes the letter.

## REVIEW

## To create a primary file

1. Type the text you want the letter to include.
2. When you want to insert a field code, click on **Tools** in the menu bar.
3. Click on the **Merge** command.
4. Click on the **Field** command.
5. Type the field name and click on the **OK** button.

Merging

195

# TASK

## Save the primary file

before

**Oops!**
If you don't want to save the file, click on the Cancel button for step 4.

1. Click on **File** in the menu bar.
   This step opens the File menu and displays a list of File commands.

2. Click on **Save**.
   This step selects the Save command. You see the Save As dialog box.

3. Type **PRIMARY.DOC**.
   This step enters the name for the primary file.

4. Click on **Save**.
   This step saves the document. The document remains open on-screen and the file name—along with the path—appears in the title bar. For more information on saving, see the tasks in the section "Managing Files."

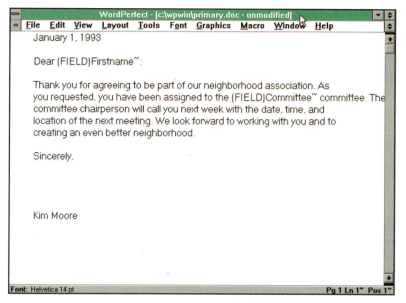
after

**Try a shortcut**
Press the Shift+F3 key combination to select the File Save command.

## REVIEW

1. Click on **File** in the menu bar.
2. Click on the **Save** command.
3. Type the file name.
4. Click on the **Save** button.

## To save the primary file

**Save again?**
To save again, select File Save. You won't be prompted for a file name. The file will be saved with the same name.

# TASK

## Merge the files

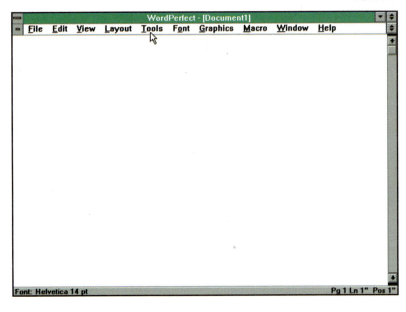

before

**Oops!**
If the merge did not go as planned, check to be sure that you typed the file names correctly. Check each of the files to be sure they are set up correctly.

1. **Open a new document.**
   To open a document, click on File and then New. See *TASK: Create a new document* for more information. The two documents will be merged and this new document will include letters for each of the records in the secondary file.

2. **Click on Tools in the menu bar.**
   This step opens the Tools menu. You see a list of Tools commands.

3. **Click on Merge.**
   This step selects the Merge command.

4. **Click on Merge.**
   This step selects the Merge command. You see the Merge dialog box; this box contains text boxes in which you type the primary and secondary file names.

5. **Type PRIMARY.DOC and press Tab.**
   This step enters the file name for the primary document.

6. **Type SECOND.DOC.**
   This step enters the file name for the secondary document.

7. **Click on OK.**
   This step merges the letters. A unique, specialized letter is created for each record in the secondary information. The text of the primary letter is the same, only for each field code, the information is pulled from the secondary file. You can print or save the letters. See *TASK: Save a document* or *TASK: Print a document*.

198

*Easy* WordPerfect for Windows

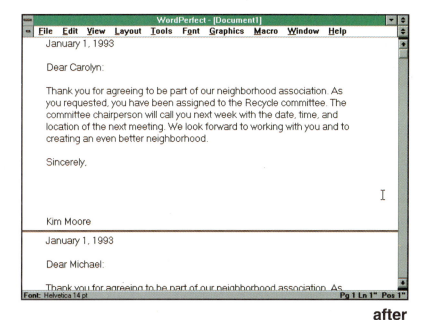

**after**

## REVIEW

### To merge the files

1. Open a new document.
2. Click on **Tools** in the menu bar.
3. Click on the **Merge** command.
4. Click on the **Merge** command.
5. Type the name of the primary file and press **Tab**.
6. Type the name of the secondary file.
7. Click on the OK button.

**A lot of options!**
The Merge feature offers a lot of options. For complete information, see *Using WordPerfect 5.2 for Windows*, Special Edition.

**Try a shortcut**
Press the Ctrl+F12 key combination to select the Merge command.

Merging  199

# Reference

Formatting Codes

Keyboard Guide

Glossary

Where To Get More Help

*Easy* WordPerfect for Windows

# Reference

## Formatting Codes

Here is a list of common formatting codes:

| Code | Meaning |
| --- | --- |
| [Bold On/Off] | Bold |
| [Center] | Center |
| [Flsh Rgt] | Flush Right |
| [Font:*name size*] | Font change |
| [HPg] | Hard Page |
| [HRt] | Hard Return |
| [Indent] | Indent |
| [Insert Pg Num: ^B] | Insert Page Number |
| [Italc On/Off] | Italic |
| [L/R Mar:#",#"] | Left/Right Margin |
| [Ln Spacing:#] | Line Spacing |
| [Pg Numbering: *position*] | Page Number |
| [SPg] | Soft Page |
| [SRt] | Soft Return |
| [Tab] | Tab |
| [Und On/Off] | Underline |

# Keyboard Guide

Instead of using the mouse with WordPerfect, you can use the keyboard. This section covers some basic keyboard operations. For complete instructions on using the keyboard, see *Using WordPerfect 5.2 for Windows,* Special Edition.

## To open a menu

Press and hold the **Alt** key, type the underlined letter in the menu name, and then release both keys. To open the

```
File
```

menu, for example, you would press **Alt+F**.

## To select a menu command

1. Use ↑ or ↓ to move to the command that you want to open.
2. Press **Enter**.

Or

Type the underlined letter in the menu command name.

## To select an option in a dialog box

Press **Tab** to move from option to option. When you access the option that you want, press the **space bar** to select that option.

You can also press and hold down the **Alt** key; type the underlined letter in the check box, text box, or list box; and then release both keys.

## To select text

Press and hold down the **Shift** key; then press the arrow keys to highlight the text in the direction of the arrow key that you are pressing. After you highlight all the text that you want, release the **Shift** key.

# Glossary

**button**  A graphic displayed in the Button Bar that lets you access a particular command. Clicking on the Close button, for example, closes the document.

**Button Bar**  An on-screen area that displays buttons you can use to access commonly used features.

**Clipboard**  A temporary storage place for text or graphics. When you cut or copy text or graphics, the item is stored in the Clipboard. The Clipboard is a Windows feature.

**Control menu icon**  The hyphen or little box that appears at the left end of the title bar of a window. Double-clicking on this box closes the window.

**default**  Standard WordPerfect settings that are in effect each time you start the program.

**dialog box**  An on-screen window that displays further command options. Many times, a dialog box reminds you of the consequences or results of a command and asks you to confirm that you want to proceed with the action.

**directory**  A list of files or an index to the files stored on disk. A directory is similar to a file cabinet; you can group files together in directories.

**document window**  The area in which you type text. You can have more than one document window open at the same time.

**DOS**  An acronym for *disk operating system*. DOS manages the details of your system—storing and retrieving programs and files.

**field**  The variable information you enter into a merge letter. You create fields in a secondary merge file.

**file**  The various individual reports, memos, databases, and letters that you store on your hard drive (or floppy disk) for future use. The actual WordPerfect program is also stored in a file.

**file name**  The name that you assign a file when you store the file to disk. A file name consists of two parts: the root and the extension. The root can be up to eight characters in length. The extension can be up to three characters in length, and it usually indicates the file type. The root and extension are separated by a period. MEMO.WPW is a valid file name. MEMO is the root, and WPW is the extension.

**floppy disk drive**  A door into your computer. The floppy disk drive enables you to put information onto the computer—onto the hard drive—and to take information off the computer—onto a floppy disk.

**font**  The style, size, and typeface of a set of characters.

**hard disk drive**  The device within your system unit that stores the programs and files with which you work. A hard disk drive is similar to a floppy disk drive, except that a hard disk stores more information, is usually not removable, and works much more quickly.

**hard return**  A code that WordPerfect inserts into a document when you press Enter. You use hard returns to end a line, end a paragraph, and insert a blank line.

**icon**  A picture that represents a group window, an application, a document, or other elements within windows.

**insertion point**  A vertical line that indicates the place where you begin typing text, deleting text, selecting text, and so on.

**menu**  An on-screen list of WordPerfect options.

**merge code**  A code that inserts a field or performs another action in a merge file.

**Microsoft Windows**  An operating environment that provides a graphical interface (rather than the character-based interface of DOS). A graphical interface enables you to learn a computer program more intuitively and to use a computer program more easily. With Microsoft Windows, you can manage your computer system—run programs, copy files, and so on.

**mouse**  An input device, like a keyboard, that allows you to move the insertion point on-screen, select menu commands, and perform other operations.

**mouse pointer**  The graphic that appears on-screen and indicates the location of the insertion point.

**path name**  The route, through directories, to a program or document file. The path C:\WPWIN\DATA\REPORT.WPW, for example, includes four elements: the disk drive (C:); the first directory (WPWIN); the subdirectory, which is a directory within the first directory (DATA); and the file name (REPORT.WPW).

**primary merge file**  One of two essential parts of a merge operation. The primary merge file contains the unchanging text of the document, as well as the merge codes that tell WordPerfect where to insert the variable information (the fields from the secondary merge file).

**record**  The collection of fields in a secondary merge file. For example, a record might store one set of information about a person.

**Reveal Codes**  A mode in which hidden codes appear on-screen. When you make formatting changes, WordPerfect inserts a hidden code into your document. When you press Tab, for example, WordPerfect inserts a [Tab] code. The term *Reveal Codes* can mean the mode in which you can see the codes or the codes themselves.

**root directory**  The main directory. The root directory contains all other directories.

**Ruler**  An on-screen graphic that enables you to make formatting changes (change tabs, fonts, line spacing, and so on). You can choose whether or not to display the Ruler.

**scroll bars**  The bars at the bottom and right of a window. Scroll arrows appear at the ends of the bars; click on the arrow to scroll the window in the direction of the arrow.

**secondary merge file**  One of two essential parts of a merge operation. The secondary merge file stores the information that you want to insert into the main document—the primary merge document. Each piece of information is stored in a *field*; a set of information is called a *record*.

**status bar**  The bottom line of the WordPerfect screen. This bar displays status indicators such as the current location of the insertion point.

**title bar**  The area of the document or application window that displays the name of the document (or application).

**window**  A rectangular area on-screen in which you view an application or a document. A window can contain icons that represent applications, the application itself, or a document you have created in an application.

**word wrap**  A WordPerfect feature that eliminates the need to press Enter each time you reach the right margin. Instead, WordPerfect moves (called *wrapping*) the word to the next line automatically.

## Where To Get More Help

This book does not cover all WordPerfect features or all ways of completing a task. This book is geared toward the beginning user—someone who wants just the basics. This person isn't ready for advanced features such as using styles or creating columns. This book covers just the most common, basic features.

As you become more comfortable with WordPerfect, you might want a more complete reference book. Que offers several WordPerfect books to suit your needs:

*Using WordPerfect 5.2 for Windows,* Special Edition

*WordPerfect 5.2 for Windows QuickStart*

*WordPerfect for Windows Quick Reference*

Also of interest:

*Easy Windows,* 3.1 Edition

*Using Windows 3.1,* Special Edition

*Windows 3.1 QuickStart*

*Windows 3.1 Quick Reference*

*Que's Computer User's Dictionary,* 3rd Edition

*Introduction to Personal Computers,* 3rd Edition

# Index

*Easy* WordPerfect for Windows

# Index

## A

abandoning changes, 70-71
activating documents, 86-87
after screens, 7
aligning text, 100-101
alphabetization, 128-129
arrows
    command names, 15
    commands, 29

## B

Backspace key, 12
backups, 20
before screens, 7
blank lines, inserting/deleting, 38-40
Bold command (Font menu), 102-103
[Bold Off] code, 102
[Bold On] code, 102
boldface text, 102-103
Button Bar, 27, 134-135, 204
Button Bar command (View menu), 134-135
buttons, 204
    Footers dialog box
        Create, 148-149
        Edit, 150-151
    Headers dialog box
        Create, 144
        Edit, 146
    Search and Replace dialog box
        Replace, 120
        Replace All, 121
        Search Next, 120
    Speller dialog box, Start, 122

## C

canceling printing, 177
cascading
    menus, 15
    windows, 85
case (text), 130-131
cells, tables, editing text, 164-165
[Center] code, 94
Center option (Line command), 94
[Center Pg] code, 152-153
center tabs, 137
centering text, 94-95, 152-153
characters, special, 156-157
check boxes, 16
checking spelling, 122-123
Clear Tabs button (Tab Set dialog box), 136-137
clicking mouse, 10
Clipboard, 54, 204
Close command (File menu), 68-69
closing
    documents after saving, 68-69
    menus, 14, 28
    windows, 32
codes, 202
    [Bold Off], 102
    [Bold On], 102
    [Center Pg], 152-153
    [Center], 94
    date, 115
    deleting, 18
    [Fig Box], 158

[Flsh Rgt] flush right, 100
[Footer], 149-150
[Header], 145-146
hidden, displaying, 18
[HLine] horizontal line, 155
[HPg] hard page break, 44
[HRt] hard return, 38
[Indent], 96, 98
[Italc Off] italic off, 106
[Italc On] italic on, 106
[Ln Spacing: n], 139
[Mar Rel] margin release, 98
merge, 206
[Pg Numbering], 143
[Tab Set], 137
[Tb Def] table definition, 162
[Und On] underline on, 104
[Und Off] underline off, 104
*see also* Reveal Codes; View codes
combining
  documents, 80-81
  paragraphs, 40-41
command buttons, 16
commands
  arrows, 15, 29
  Edit menu
    Convert Case, 130-131
    Copy, 54-55
    Cut, 52, 56-57
    Go To, 46-47
    Paste, 52-53
    Replace, 118-121
    Search, 116-117
    Select, 48-49
    Undelete, 52-53
    Undo, 34
  ellipsis (...), 15, 29

File menu
  Close, 68-69
  New, 76-77
  Open, 72-75, 82-83
  Print, 174-177
  Print Preview, 170-171
  Retrieve, 80-81
  Save, 62-65, 78-79, 190-191, 196-197
  Save As, 66-67
  Select Printer, 168-169
Font menu
  Bold, 102-103
  Font, 108-111
  Italic, 106-107
  Underline, 104-105
  WP Characters, 156-157
Graphics menu
  Figure, 158-159
  Line, 154-155
Layout menu
  Line, 94-95, 100-101, 136-139
  Margins, 140-141
  Page, 44, 142-153
  Paragraph, 96-99
  Tables, 162-163
menus, selecting, 14-17, 28-29
Program Manager
  Exit Windows, 30-31
selecting with keyboard, 203
Tools menu
  Date, 114-115
  Merge, 182-183, 186-189, 192-195, 198-199
  Sort, 128-129
  Speller, 122-123
  Thesaurus, 124-125
  Word Count, 126-127

# Index

View menu
  Button Bar, 134-135
  Draft mode, 172-173
  Reveal Codes, 17, 92-93
  Ruler, 132-133
Window menu
  Tile, 84-85
computer, turning on, 26
Control menu icon, 204
Convert Case command (Edit menu), 130-131
Copy command (Edit menu), 54
copying text, 54-55
counting words, 126-127
Create button
  Footers dialog box, 148-149
  Headers dialog box, 144
Create option, Tables command (Layout menu), 162-163
Create Table dialog box, 162-163
creating
  documents, 76-77
  files
    primary, 181, 192-195
    secondary, 180-185
  footers, 148-149
  headers, 144-145
  merge letters, 180-181
current directory, 74
cursor position indicator (Pos), 14
Cut command (Edit menu), 52-53, 56-57

## D

Date command (Tools menu), 114-115
dates
  codes, 115
  format, default, 114-115
  inserting, 114-115
  prompt, 26
  updating, 115
decimal tabs, 137
defaults, 204
  date format, 114-115
  fonts, 109
  tab settings, 137
  tabs, 42-43
Del key, 12
deleting
  codes, 18
  fields, merge files, 193, 195
  files, 88-89
  footers, 149
  headers, 145
  lines, 38, 40, 155
  page breaks, 44
  records, secondary files, 189
  tabs, 42, 137
  text, 34, 50-53
dialog boxes, 15, 204
  check boxes, 16
  command buttons, 17
  Create Table, 162-163
  File Open, 72
  Font, 108-109
  Footers, 148-149
  Go To, 46-47
  Headers, 144-147
  Horizontal Line, 154-155
  Insert Merge Codes, 182-183, 192-193
  list boxes, 16
  Margins, 140-141
  Merge, 198-199

Merge Codes, 184-185
Open File, 74-75, 88-89
options
  buttons, 17
  selecting with keyboard, 203
Print, 174-177
Retrieve Figure, 158-159
Retrieve File, 80-81
Save As, 62, 66, 190-191
Save Selected Text, 78-79
Search, 116
Search and Replace, 118
Select Printer, 168-169
Sort, 128-129
Spacing, 138-139
Speller, 122
Tab Set, 136-137
text boxes, 16
Thesaurus, 124-125
Undelete, 52
Word Count, 126-127
directories, 204
  current, 74
  files, displaying, 74-75
  parent, 74
  path name, 206
  root, 207
disk operating system, *see* DOS
displaying
  Button Bar, 134-135
  codes, hidden, 18
  documents
    Draft mode, 172-173
    multiple, 84-85
  files, directories, 74-75
  Reveal Codes, 92-93
  Ruler, 132-133

document screen, 13
  document window, 13
  menu bar, 13
  status bar, 14
  title bar, 13
document window, 13, 19, 204
documents
  activating, 86-87
  combining, 80-81
  creating, 76-77
  date, updating, 115
  displaying
    Draft mode, 172-173
    multiple, 84-85
  editing, abandoning changes, 70-71
  inserting in documents, 81
  moving to top, 47
  opening, 72-73, 82-83
  printing, 170-171, 174-175
  saving, 62-63
    and closing, 68-69
    new name, 66-67
    resaving, 64-65
DOS (disk operating system), 204
dot leaders, 137
double line spacing, 138-139
Draft mode (View menu), 172-173
drag and drop, moving text, 57
dragging mouse, 10
drawing lines, 154-155
drivers, printers, 168-169
drives
  changing, 75
  disks, 205

# Index

## E

Edit button
  Footers dialog box, 150-151
  Headers dialog box, 146-147
Edit menu commands
  Convert Case, 130-131
  Copy, 54-55
  Cut, 52-53, 56-57
  Go To, 46-47
  Paste, 52-53
  Replace, 118-121
  Search, 116-117
  Select, 48-49
  Undelete, 52-53
  Undo, 34, 58-59
editing
  documents, abandoning changes, 70-71
  footers, 150-151
  headers, 146-147
  text, cells, tables, 164-165
ellipsis (...) in commands, 15, 29
Esc key, 12
exercises, explanation, 4-5
Exit command, 28
Exit Windows command, Program Manager, 30-31
exiting WordPerfect, 27, 30-31

## F

Field Name text box (Merge Codes dialog box), 184-185
Field option (Merge command [Tools menu]), 192-195
fields, 182-183, 193-195, 204
[Fig Box] code, 158
Figure command (Graphics menu), 158-159
File menu
  commands
    Close, 68-69
    New, 76-77
    Open, 72-75, 82-83
    Print, 174-177
    Print Preview, 170-171
    Retrieve, 80-81
    Save, 62-65, 78-79, 190-191, 196-197
    Save As, 66-67
    Select Printer, 168-169
  opening, 28
file names, 205
File Open dialog box, 72
Filename text box, 74
files, 205
  deleting, 88-89
  displaying, directories, 74-75
  merging, 198-199
  paths, 62
  primary, 206
    creating, 181, 192-195
    saving, 196-197
  saving, replacing, 63
  secondary, 207
    creating, 180-185
    saving, 190-191
floppy disk drive, 205
[Flsh Rgt] flush right code, 100
Flush Right option (Line command), 100-101
flush right text alignment, 100-101
following exercises, 4-5

Font command (Font menu), 108-111
Font dialog box
  Font list, 108-109
  Point Size list, 110-111
Font list (Font dialog box), 108-109
Font menu commands
  Bold, 102-103
  Font, 108-111
  Italic, 106-107
  Underline, 104-105
  WP Characters, 156-157
fonts, 108-109
  default, 109
  disks, 205
  Iconic Symbols, 156-157
  listing, 108-109
  size, 110-111
[Footer] code, 149-150
Footer window, 148-151
footers
  creating, 148-149
  deleting, 149
  editing, 150-151
  page numbers, 149
  text, formatting, 151
Footers dialog box
  Create button, 148-149
  Edit button, 150-151
Footers option (Page command [Layout menu]), 148-151
formatting
  codes, 92-93, 202
  dates, default, 114-115
  Ruler, 132-133
  text
    footers, 151
    headers, 147
  *see also* Reveal Codes

Full Page option (Print Preview command [File menu]), 170-171
function keys, 11-12

## G

Go To command (Edit menu), 46-47
Go To dialog box, 46
graphics
  Clipboard, 204
  inserting, 158-159
  moving, 160-161
Graphics menu commands
  Figure, 158-159
  Line, 154-155
group icons, WordPerfect for Windows, 26

## H

Hanging Indent option (Paragraph command), 98
hanging indents, 98
hard code, [HRt], 38
hard disk drive, 205
hard page breaks, 44-45
hard return, 39, 205
hardware requirements, 5
[Header] code, 145-146
Header window, 144-145, 147
headers
  creating, 144-145
  deleting, 145
  editing, 146-147
  page numbers, 145-147
  text, formatting, 147
Headers dialog box, 145
  Create button, 144
  Edit button, 146-147

# Index

Headers option (Page command [Layout menu]), 144-147
Help
  menu, opening, 32
  topics, 32
  window, closing, 32
hidden codes, displaying, 18
[HLine] horizontal line code, 155
Horizontal Line dialog box, 154-155
horizontal lines, drawing, 154-155
Horizontal option (Line command [Graphics menu]), 154-155
[HPg] hard page break code, 44
[HRt] hard return code, 38

## I

Iconic Symbols font set, 156-157
icons, 205
  Control menu, 204
  groups, WordPerfect for Windows, 26
  program, WordPerfect for Windows, 27
[Indent] code, 96, 98
Indent command (Paragraph option), 96-97
indenting text, 43, 96-98
Ins key, 12, 36
Insert Merge Codes dialog box, 182-183, 192-193
inserting
  characters, 156-157
  date, 114-115
  documents in documents, 81
  graphics, 158-159
  lines, blank, 38-39
  tables, 162-163
  tabs, 42-43
insertion point, 205
  moving
    with keyboard, 16-17
    with mouse, 16
  moving to, 46
  placing, 36
  selecting text, 48
  unmoving, 13
installing WordPerfect, 27
[Italc Off] italic off code, 106
[Italc On] italic on code, 106
Italic command (Font menu), 106-107
italics, 106-107

## K

keyboard, 11-12
  function keys, 11-12
  modifier keys, 12
  moving insertion point, 16-17
  opening menus, 203
  repeating keys, 12
  selecting
    commands, 203
    options, dialog boxes, 203
    text, 49, 203
  special keys, 12
keyboard shortcuts, 12
  Alt+Backspace (undo), 59
  Alt+F1 (Thesaurus), 125
  Alt+F3 (Reveal Codes), 93
  Alt+F7 (Flush Right), 101
  Alt+Shift+F3 (Ruler), 133
  Ctrl+B (Bold), 103

Ctrl+Enter (Hard Page Break), 45
Ctrl+F1 (Speller), 123
Ctrl+F2 (Replace), 119
Ctrl+F4 (File Close), 69
Ctrl+F5 (Date Text), 115
Ctrl+F8 (Margins), 141
Ctrl+F12 (Merge), 183
Ctrl+G (Go To), 47
Ctrl+Home (Go To Top of Document), 47
Ctrl+I (Italics), 107
Ctrl+Ins (Copy), 55
Ctrl+Shift+F7 (Double Indent), 97
Ctrl+Shift+F12 (Sort), 129
Ctrl+U (Underline), 105
Ctrl+W (WP Characters), 157
F2 (Search), 117
F3 (Save As), 67
F4 (File Open), 73
F5 (Print), 175
F7 (Indent), 97
F9 (Font), 109, 111
Shift+F3 (File Save), 63, 191
Shift+F4 (File New), 77
Shift+F5 (Print Preview), 171
Shift+F7 (Center), 95
Shift+Ins (Paste), 55
keyboards

## L

Layout menu commands
   Line, 94-95, 100-101, 136-139
   Margins, 140-141
   Page, 44-45, 142-153
   Paragraph, 96-99
   Tables, 162-163
letters, merge, *see* merge letters
Line command (Graphics menu), 154-155
Line command (Layout menu), 100-101
   options
      Center, 94-95
      Flush Right, 100-101
      Spacing, 138-139
      Tab Set, 136-137
line number indicator (Ln), 14
line-spacing, double, 138-139
lines (drawing)
   deleting, 155
   horizontal, 154-155
lines (text)
   blank, 38-40
   deleting, 155
list boxes, 16
listing fonts, 108-109
Ln (line number indicator), 14
[Ln Spacing: *n*] code, 139

## M

[Mar Rel] margin release code, 98
margin notes, 7
margins, setting, 140-141
Margins command (Layout menu), 140-141
Margins dialog box, 140-141
menu bar, 13
menus, 205
   cascading, 15
   closing, 14, 28

# Index

commands, selecting, 10, 14-17, 28-29, 203
opening, keyboard, 203
merge codes, 206
Merge Codes dialog box, 184-185
Merge Codes subcommand (Tools menu), 182-183
Merge command (Tools menu), 186-189, 192-195
    Merge Codes subcommand, 182-183
    options
        Field, 192-195
        Merge, 198-199
Merge dialog box, 198-199
merge letters
    fields, 182-183, 204-205
    records, 180-181
    *see also* primary files; secondary files
Merge option (Merge command [Tools menu]), 198-199
merging, 180-181, 198-199
Microsoft Windows, 206
modifier keys, 12
monitors, 26
mouse, 10, 206
    clicking, 10
    dragging, 10
    moving insertion point, 17
    pointer, 10, 206
    pointing, 10
    selecting commands, 10
moving
    graphics, 160-161
    insertion point
        with keyboard, 16-17
        with mouse, 16

pointers, mouse, 10
text, 56-57
to insertion point, 46
to pages, 46-47
top of document, 47

## N

naming documents, 66-67
New command (File menu), 76-77
Numbering option (Page command [Layout menu]), 142-143
numbering pages, 142-143
    footers, 149
    headers, 145, 147

## O

Oops! notes, 6
Open command (File menu), 72-75, 82-83
Open File dialog box
    deleting files, 88-89
    Filename text box, 74
opening
    documents, 72-73, 82-83
    File menu, 28
    Help menu, 32
    menus, keyboard, 203
option buttons, 17
options
    Convert Case command, 130-131
    Date command (Tools menu), 114-115
    dialog boxes, selecting with keyboard, 203
    Figure command (Graphics menu), 158-159

Line command (Graphics menu), Horizontal, 154-155
Line command (Layout menu)
　Center, 94
　Flush Right, 100-101
　Spacing, 138-139
　Tab Set, 136-137
Merge command (Tools menu)
　Field, 192-195
　Merge, 198-199
Page command (Layout menu)
　Footers, 148-151
　Headers, 144-147
　Numbering, 142-143
Paragraph command
　Hanging Indent, 98
　Indent, 96-97
Print Preview command (File menu), Full Page, 170-171
Tables command (Layout menu), Create, 162-163
overlapping windows, 85
overwriting text, 35-37

## P

page breaks, 44-45
　deleting, 44
　hard, 44-45
　soft, 45
Page command (Layout menu), 44, 142-143, 152-153
　options
　　Footers, 148-151
　　Headers, 144-147
　　Numbering, 142-143
page number indicator (Pg), 14
page numbering, 142-143
　footers, 149
　headers, 145-147
pages, moving to, 46-47
Paragraph command (Layout menu), 96-98
　options
　　Hanging Indent, 98
　　Indent, 96-97
paragraphs
　combining, 40-41
　splitting, 40
parent directory, 74
Paste command (Edit menu), 52
path name, 206
paths, 62
[Pg Numbering] code, 143
Pg (page number indicator), 14
Point Size list (Font dialog box), 110-111
pointers, mouse, 10, 206
Pos (cursor position) indicator, 14
previewing documents, 170-171
primary files, 206
　creating, 181, 192-195
　fields, deleting, 193-195
　saving, 196-197
Print command (File menu), 174-177
Print dialog box, 174-177
Print Preview command (File menu), 170-171

# Index

printers
  drivers, 168-169
  selecting, 168-169
printing
  canceling, 177
  documents, 174-175
  previewing, 170-171
  printers, selecting, 168-169
  text, selected, 176-177
program icons, WordPerfect for Windows, 27
Program Manager, 26, 30-31
prompts, 26

## R

records, secondary files, 180-181, 186-189, 206
Relative Position text box (Tab Set dialog box), 136-137
repeating
  keys, 12
  searches, 117
Replace All button (Search and Replace dialog box), 121
Replace button (Search and Replace dialog box), 120
Replace command (Edit menu), 118-121
Replace With text box
  Search and Replace dialog box, 118
  Speller dialog box, 122
replacing
  files, saving, 63
  spelling words, 122
  text, 37, 118-121
requirements, hardware/software, 5

resaving documents, 64-65
resizing windows, Reveal Codes, 93
restarting WordPerfect, 30-31
restoring text, 50, 52–53
Retrieve command (File menu), 80-81
Retrieve Figure dialog box, 158-159
Retrieve File dialog box, 80
Retrieve option (Figure command [Graphics menu]), 158-159
retrieving, 19-20
  text, selected, 79
returns
  end of paragraph, 40
  hard, 39
  soft, 39
Reveal Codes, 18-19, 206
  displaying, 92-93
  window, resizing, 93
Reveal Codes command (View menu), 18, 92-93
reverse video, 48
reversing changes, 36
review sections, 7
right tabs, 137
root directory, 207
Ruler, 27, 132-133, 207
Ruler command (View menu), 132-133

## S

Save As command (File menu), 66-67
Save As dialog box, 62, 66, 190-191

Save command (File menu), 62-65, 78-79, 190-191, 196-197
Save Selected Text dialog box, 78-79
saving, 19-20
　backups, 20
　documents, 62-63
　　and closing, 68-69
　　new name, 66-67
　　resaving, 64-65
　files
　　primary, 196-197
　　replacing, 63
　　secondary, 190-191
　text, selected, 78-79
screens
　before/after, 7
　document, *see* document screen
scroll bars, 207
Search and Replace dialog box
　buttons
　　Replace, 120
　　Replace All, 121
　　Search Next, 120
　text boxes
　　Replace With, 118
　　Search for, 118
Search command (Edit menu), 116-117
Search dialog box, 116
Search for text box, 118
Search Next button (Search and Replace dialog box), 120
search strings, 116, 118
searching
　for text, 116-121
　repeating, 117
secondary files, 207
　creating, 180-185
　records, 186-189
　saving, 190-191
Select command (Edit menu), 48
Select Printer command (File menu), 168-169
Select Printer dialog box, 168-169
selecting
　check boxes, 16
　command button, 17
　commands
　　menus, 14-17, 28-29, 203
　　mouse, 10
　list boxes, 16
　option buttons, 17
　options, dialog boxes, with keyboard, 203
　printers, 168-169
　text, 48-49
　　counting words, 127
　　insertion point, 48
　　keyboard, 49
　　printing, 176-177
　　retrieving, 79
　　saving, 78-79
　　with keyboard, 203
　text boxes, 16
setting
　margins, 140-141
　tabs, 136-137
Shift key, 12
shortcuts, *see* keyboard shortcuts
size, fonts, 110-111
soft page breaks, 45
soft returns, 39

# Index

software requirements, 5
Sort command (Tools menu), 128-129
Sort dialog box, 128-129
sorting text, 128-129
spacing lines, 138-139
Spacing dialog box, 138-139
Spacing option (Line command), 138-139
special characters, inserting, 156-157
special keys, 12
Speller command (Tools menu), 122-123
Speller dialog box, 122
spelling check, 122-123
splitting paragraphs, 40
Start button (Speller dialog box), 122
starting WordPerfect, 26-27, 30-31
status bar, 14, 207
   Ln (line number inches), 14
   Pg (page number indicator), 14
   Pos (cursor position) indicator, 14
strings, search, 116-118

## T

[Tab Set] code, 137
Tab Set dialog box, 136-137
   Clear Tabs button, 136-137
   text boxes, Relative Position, 136-137
Tab Set option (Line command), 136-137
tables
   cells, editing text, 164-165
   inserting, 162-163
   text, entering, 164-165
Tables command (Layout menu), 162-163
tabs
   center, 137
   decimal, 137
   default, 42
   deleting, 42, 137
   dot leaders, 137
   inserting, 42-43
   right, 137
   setting, 136-137
tasks, 6
   margin notes, 7
   screens, before/after, 7
[Tb Def] table definition code, 162
text
   aligning, 100-101
   boldface, 102-103
   case, 130-131
   centering, 94-95, 152-153
   copying, 54-55
   deleting, 34, 50-53
   editing, cells, tables, 164-165
   formatting
      footers, 151
      headers, 147
   indenting, 43, 96-98
   italics, 106-107
   moving, 56-57
   overwriting, 35-37
   replacing, 37
   searching for, 116-121
   selecting, 48-49

counting words, 127
insertion point, 48
keyboard, 49
printing, 176-177
retrieving, 79
saving, 78-79
with keyboard, 203
sorting, 128-129
tables, entering, 164-165
typing, 18, 34-35
underlining, 104-105
Text option (Date command), 114-115
thesaurus, 124-125
Thesaurus command (Tools menu), 124-125
Thesaurus dialog box, 124-125
Tile command (Window menu), 84-85
tiling windows, 84-85
time prompt, 26
title bar, 13, 207
Tools menu commands
   Date, 114-115
   Merge, 182-183, 186-189, 192-195, 198-199
   Sort, 128-129
   Speller, 122-123
   Thesaurus, 124-125
   Word Count, 126-127
topics (help), 32
turning on/off computer, 26
typeover mode, 35-36
typing text, 18, 34-35

## U–V

[Und Off] underline off code, 104
[Und On] underline on code, 104
Undelete command (Edit menu), 52
Undelete dialog box, 52
Underline command (Font menu), 104-105
underlining, 104-105
Undo, 58-59
Undo command (Edit menu), 34, 58
undoing, 36
Uppercase option (Convert Case command), 130-131
View menu commands
   Button Bar, 134-135
   Draft mode, 172-173
   Reveal Codes, 18, 92-93
   Ruler, 132-133

## W–Z

Window menu commands, 84-85
windows, 207
   cascading, 85
   document, 204
   document, *see* document window
   Footer, 148-151
   Header, 144-147
   Help, closing, 32
   overlapping, 85
   Reveal Codes, 18, 93
   scroll bars, 207
   tiling, 84-85

# Index

Word Count, 126-127
Word Count command (Tools menu), 126-127
Word Count dialog box, 126-127
Word text box (Thesaurus dialog box), 124-125
word wrap, 18, 39, 207
WordPerfect
 exiting, 27, 30-31
 installing, 27
 restarting, 30-31
 starting, 26-27
WordPerfect for Windows
 group icon, 26
 icons, program, 27
WP Characters command (Font menu), 156-157